THE AESTHETIC APPRECIATION OF NATURE

The Aesthetic Appreciation of Nature

Essays on the Aesthetics of Nature

Malcolm Budd

CLARENDON PRESS · OXFORD

OXFORD

UNIVERSITY PRESS

Great Clarendon Street, Oxford OX2 6DP

Oxford University Press is a department of the University of Oxford.
It furthers the University's objective of excellence in research, scholarship,
and education by publishing worldwide in

Oxford New York

Auckland Bangkok Buenos Aires Cape Town Chennai
Dar es Salaam Delhi Hong Kong Istanbul Karachi Kolkata
Kuala Lumpur Madrid Melbourne Mexico City Mumbai Nairobi
São Paulo Shanghai Taipei Tokyo Toronto

Oxford is a registered trade mark of Oxford University Press
in the UK and in certain other countries

Published in the United States
by Oxford University Press Inc., New York

© in this volume Malcolm Budd 2002

The moral rights of the author have been asserted

Database right Oxford University Press (maker)

First published 2002

British Library Cataloguing in Publication Data

Data available

Library of Congress Cataloging in Publication Data

Budd, Malcolm, 1941–
The aesthetic appreciation of nature : essays on the aesthetics of
nature / Malcolm Budd.
p. cm.
Includes bibliographical references and index.
1. Nature (Aesthetics) 1. Title
BH301.N3 B83 2002   111'.85—dc21   2002029843
ISBN 0-19-925965-8

1 3 5 7 9 10 8 6 4 2

Typeset by Kolam Information Services Pvt. Ltd., Pondicherry, India
Printed in Great Britain on acid-free paper by
Biddles Ltd., Guildford & Kings Lynn

The more I study Nature, the more I become impressed with ever increasing force, that the contrivances and beautiful adaptations slowly acquired through each part occasionally varying to a slight degree but in many ways, with the preservation of those variations which were beneficent to the organism under complex and ever varying conditions of life, transcend, in an incomparable manner, the contrivances and adaptations which the most fertile imagination of men could invent.

Charles Darwin

> Therefore am I still
> A lover of the meadows and the woods
> And mountains; and of all that we behold
> From this green earth; of all the mighty world
> Of eye and ear, both what they half create,
> And what perceive; well pleased to recognise
> In nature and the language of the sense
> The anchor of my purest thoughts, the nurse,
> The guide, the guardian of my heart, and soul
> Of all my moral being.

William Wordsworth, 'Lines Composed
a Few Miles above Tintern Abbey'

PREFACE

Prior to the last decades of the twentieth century there had been little serious philosophical reflection on the aesthetics of nature. Before that time, in the entire history of western philosophy, notwithstanding the insights that can be found in the works of Addison, Burke, Hume, Schopenhauer, Hegel, and Santayana, for example, there had been just one major contribution to the subject, that of Immanuel Kant. Kant's contribution dwarfs all previous thought and it has not been followed by anything of comparable rank: it is the only philosophical writing on the aesthetic appreciation of nature by a major figure that rewards sustained attention. A paper by Ronald Hepburn in the late 1960s breathed new life into the subject, encouraging at first a trickle of publications which has now developed into a veritable flood.

The peculiar history of the subject is reflected in the character of this book. It collects four essays on the aesthetics of nature published in the last six years, each of which is almost entirely self-contained, so that they can be read independently of one another and in any order, but which complement one another by exploring the topic from different points of view.

The first essay opens with the declaration of a somewhat demanding conception of how the idea of the aesthetic appreciation of nature should be understood—as the aesthetic appreciation of nature *as* nature—a conception that invites the question whether there can be such a thing. This conception is developed by an elucidation of, first, the idea of the object of appreciation; that is, nature. This covers both pristine nature and nature affected by humanity, and I consider the consequences of humanity's intrusions into nature on the aesthetic appreciation of nature as so affected. The second development of my conception of the aesthetic appreciation of nature concerns the subject of appreciation—the subject's response to nature as nature. Here I distinguish two ways in which this might be understood, one of which might provoke scepticism about the possibility of aesthetically appreciating nature as nature. I defuse this scepticism by, first, emphasizing the significance of the way in which our perception of the world is informed by the concepts under which we bring whatever we see and, second, proposing an account of what constitutes an aesthetic response to something. These developments enable me to illustrate how the demands imposed by the strongest form of my conception of the aesthetic appreciation of nature can be met—sometimes, not always. Given that how we see the world, what we see it as being, can affect how we respond to it, the question arises of what knowledge, if any, is essential to the aesthetic appreciation of nature, and the essay concludes by exploring the aesthetic relevance of knowledge of nature and how it might enhance (or diminish) aesthetic appreciation.

The second essay, which has been split into three parts, is a comprehensive exposition and examination of Kant's mature thoughts about aesthetic delight in the natural world. Although the account it presents of Kant's thought is, I believe, sound—even the eminently contestable interpretation of Kant's leading idea in his account of the mathematically sublime—it is not an exercise in that form of scholarship for which the sole or primary concern is to elucidate Kant's texts and to defend the proposed interpretation of them against rival interpretations. What I have chosen to do is to present Kant's principal thoughts about the aesthetic appreciation of nature as I believe they should be understood and to subject them to criticism where that seems necessary. There is a great deal to be learnt from Kant's work, and an uncluttered presentation with an accompanying evaluation seems to me to be the most profitable way of reaping the benefits of Kant's thoughts. I have tried to write in such a way as to minimize the demands on a reader whose knowledge of Kant's writings is relatively limited, although these demands will nevertheless occasionally be considerable.

The third essay focuses on what is distinctive of the aesthetics of nature. I begin by arguing against its assimilation to the aesthetics of art by attempting to demonstrate the inadequacy of the view that the aesthetic appreciation of nature should be understood as the appreciation of nature as if it were art. This leads to an examination of three theses. The first maintains that from the aesthetic point of view natural items should be appreciated under concepts of the natural things or phenomena they are. The second asserts that what aesthetic properties a natural item actually possesses are determined by which categories of nature the item should be experienced as belonging to. The third—the doctrine of positive aesthetics with respect to nature—claims that the aesthetics of pristine nature, unlike that of art, must be entirely positive, nature unaffected by humanity being such as to make judgements of negative aesthetic value about the products of the natural world misplaced. In conclusion, I attempt to show that the idea of the aesthetic value of a natural item is such that it endows the aesthetic appreciation of nature with a freedom and relativity denied to the appreciation of art and renders the doctrine of positive aesthetics, which can assume many forms, problematic.

The final essay is a critical survey of many, but certainly not all, of the issues discussed and the positions put forward in the literature that has followed the publication of Hepburn's paper. These ongoing discussions, many of them initiated by a series of challenging papers by Allen Carlson, have, I believe, greatly advanced the subject. My essay is not intended as just a guide through the literature: what I have set myself to do is to distinguish the wheat from the chaff and to highlight unresolved problems.

A recurring theme of the essays is that the right way to experience nature aesthetically is to respond to it *as being nature*. This mode of response, which can be realized in many different ways and in stronger or weaker forms, has immense advantages over both of its main rivals, each of which is inadequately motivated. The formalist conception of the aesthetic appreciation of nature, which focuses exclusively upon the character nature presents when considered in abstraction from the concepts under which it might be experienced by observers who have greater or lesser knowledge of what kinds of natural item they are perceiving, is unnecessarily restrictive and, accordingly, impoverishing. The view that the aesthetic experience of nature consists in regarding nature as if it were art imposes an alien model on the aesthetic appreciation of nature (under the illusion that there is no natural or viable alternative) and, in advocating that we regard nature as what we know it not to be, licenses the most fanciful interpretations of nature and wrongly denies the possibility of straightforwardly true, non-relative judgements of the aesthetic properties and value of natural things—judgements that are not relative to whatever idiosyncratic way of conceiving of nature an observer might choose to adopt. In different ways, both positions refuse to recognize nature as being what nature actually is. In contrast, the view I recommend embraces, welcomes, and may even glorify, the true character of nature and, in doing so, ushers in an enormous enrichment of the aesthetic experience of nature whilst allowing that aesthetic judgements about nature can be plainly true. At the same time I clip the wings of more extravagant versions of the natural aesthetic I favour that seem to me to over-emphasize the role of scientific knowledge in the aesthetic appreciation of nature.

The essays have been revised, and in some places greatly added to, since they were first published. Inevitably, some issues come up more than once: when this happens I have minimized the overlap by, first, compressing the later treatment and introducing some new points if the earlier treatment is reasonably comprehensive, and, second, expanding the later treatment of aspects of an issue given short shrift earlier.

I am grateful to the Oxford University Press for permission to make use of my 'The Aesthetic Appreciation of Nature' and 'Delight in the Natural World: Kant on the Aesthetic Appreciation of Nature', originally published in *The British Journal of Aesthetics*, 36/2 (July 1996) and 38/1–3 (January–July 1998), which form the basis of the first two essays, and for allowing me to publish as the final essay a considerably expanded version of 'Aesthetics of Nature' from the *Oxford Handbook of Aesthetics*. The third essay is a little-changed version of 'The Aesthetics of Nature', which originally appeared in the *Proceedings of the Aristotelian Society*, vol. C, pt. 2 (2000). Material from this article is reprinted by courtesy of the Editor of the *Aristotelian Society* © 2003, for which I am grateful.

M. J. B.
Cambridge, May 2002

CONTENTS

xii   *Contents*

I

The Aesthetic Appreciation of Nature as Nature

Die liebe Erde allüberall
Blüht auf im Lenz und grünt aufs neu!
Allüberall und ewig blauen licht die Fernen!

Gustav Mahler, *Das Lied von der Erde*[1]

1.1. THE AESTHETIC APPRECIATION OF NATURE AS NATURE

What is it to appreciate nature aesthetically? Is there such a thing as the aesthetic appreciation of nature? These questions refer, on the one hand, to an object and, on the other, to a type of appreciation: the object is nature and the type is aesthetic. So an illuminating response must do two things: it must provide both a delimitation of the field of nature and an account of what constitutes the aesthetic appreciation of items in that field. The first element of such a response might appear to be independent of the second. But in fact the relevant understanding of the concept of nature cannot be determined by putting aesthetic considerations entirely to one side: the desired distinction between the natural and the non-natural can be drawn only by bearing in mind the purpose for which it is required. And the second element must be informed by the first, for the aesthetic appreciation of nature, as I understand the idea, is the aesthetic appreciation of nature *as nature*. It follows that, in my understanding of the notion, not every aesthetic experience available from a natural object is an instance of the aesthetic appreciation of nature. The aesthetic appreciation of nature is not coextensive with the set of aesthetic responses to natural objects or to aspects of what

[1] 'The beloved earth everywhere blossoms in spring and turns green again! Everywhere and eternally the distance shines bright and blue!'

is found in nature. Rather, an aesthetic response to something natural constitutes aesthetic appreciation of nature only if the response is a response to nature *as* nature, and what this requires is that it must be integral to the rewarding (or displeasing) character of the experience offered by nature that its object is experienced *as* natural. Hence, if some expanse of an attractive shade of colour presented by an out-crop of ochre delights, but not *as* a natural colour or *as* the colour of a natural object, or a pattern in a snowflake delights, but not *as* naturally produced, or the iridescent colours of a hummingbird delight, but not *as* the appearance of its wings, although the experi-ence is aesthetic and provided by nature, it is not an instance of the aesthetic appreciation of nature. Of course, this is not the only way of understanding the idea of the aesthetic appreciation of nature, which might instead be understood to mean no more than the aesthetic appreciation of anything that is available in nature for aesthetic appreciation—any natural thing or phenomenon that is susceptible of aesthetic appreciation. Furthermore, there is no purely aesthetic requirement that a natural thing should be appreciated aesthetically as the natural thing it is or as being a thing of a certain natural kind or just as being a natural thing; and it may well be aesthetically more rewarding not to do so but to contemplate it in abstraction from whatever kind it is seen to be and focus on its shape, textures, and colouring. But just as artistic appreciation is the appreciation of art *as* art, so the aesthetic appreciation of nature should be understood to demand the appreciation of nature as nature.

1.2.   THE IDEA OF NATURE

But if an aesthetic response to something natural constitutes aes-thetic appreciation of nature only if the response is a response to nature *as* nature, what is meant by nature and how should the idea of nature, as it figures in the aesthetic appreciation of nature, be correctly thought of?[2]

In one sense, everything is a part of nature, for there is a sense in which nature is just the totality of everything that is the case.

---

[2] In a different context David Hume wrote: 'our answer to this question depends upon the definition of the word, Nature, than which there is none more ambiguous and equivocal' (Hume 1960: bk. III, pt. I, §II).

But this all-inclusive sense does not distinguish nature from anything else, and what is needed is a distinction within nature, when nature is understood in this all-embracing sense as 'the world'.

What does nature consist of? Well, there are natural substances (gold, water), natural species (animals, insects, trees, shrubs, plants), natural objects (icebergs, mountains, volcanoes, planets, moons), natural forces (gravity, magnetism), natural appearances (the sky, sunrise and sunset, a rainbow, shadows), natural phenomena (rivers, wind, rain, snow, clouds), natural products of living things (bird-song, beaver dams, birds' nests, spiders' webs, faeces, the smell of a rose), and so on. But in one sense nature consists of individual natural things standing in relations to one another. These things are instances of natural kinds—natural species and natural 'substances'—and they interact through the operation of natural forces. So in nature there are, on the one hand, individual spatio-temporal items, and, on the other, the types that they instantiate and the forces under the influence of which they affect one another. But what makes any of these things natural?

Natural objects are often contrasted with man-made objects, even in the case of artefacts that are made out of natural objects merely by modifying them. But the distinction between what is man-made[3] and what is not will divide the world into the natural and the non-natural only if the idea of art or skill is built into the idea of making, and perhaps not even then. For human beings make other human beings, usually by natural means, not by art or skill and often not with the intention of doing so, and the human body remains a natural object no matter how it may be clothed, or shaped, or coloured by human design. But in so far as it is a human artefact (usually a self-artefact), it is a natural item stamped with human activity, even if not 'aestheticized' by human design. In one sense, what makes a human body a natural object—whether it has been produced naturally or by artificial means—is the fact that its principle of growth as it endures through time is a matter of nature, not human contrivance: as with certain other kinds of natural objects, trees, for example, all living things, indeed, the pattern of growth of human bodies is inherent in them. So what is natural should not be thought of as what is 'human

---

[3] 'Man-made' is here understood not only in a gender-free sense, but as including anything made by another, non-human, intelligent species as a result of a decision to do so, if there should be such a species in the universe.

neither in itself nor its origins',[4] and it should be opposed not to
what is man-made but to what is artefactual (a work of human
artifice).[5] This opposition between the natural and the artefactual
captures the prime meaning of the idea of nature as it figures in the
aesthetic appreciation of nature, although there are complications
that are occasioned by the fact that an object of observation can be,
in a number of different ways, partly natural, partly artefactual, and
something that is a natural *object* might nevertheless not be in a
natural *state*.

So the aesthetic appreciation of nature (as nature) needs to be
distinguished from the appreciation of nature as artefact. But this
presupposes—what I take to be the truth—that nature is not an
artefact, an assumption denied by theists, who believe nature to be
God's creation. Now those who have regarded nature as an artefact
of God and have delighted aesthetically in it *as* such a creation, so
that their appreciation is permeated by the idea of it as the creation
of God, appreciate nature as an artefact (but not thereby as a work
of art, unless it is God's revealed intention that it should be recognized as designed for such appreciation). If the aesthetic appreciation of nature is understood to require that nature is not seen as an
artefact, this would appear to rule that the aesthetic appreciation of
nature as an artefact of God falls outside the aesthetic appreciation
of nature as nature; but an artefact is normally something made
from what is present in nature, and the creation of nature *ex nihilo*,
rather than from pre-existing natural things, might well be thought,
in virtue of its exceptional character, to fall outside the requirement.
Nevertheless, the aesthetic appreciation of nature as an artefact of
God conceives of nature as being designed, and inasmuch as God's
design is read into nature its appreciation differs in a crucial respect
from the aesthetic appreciation of nature as nature, not as artefact.
In fact, if God is conceived of as being all-powerful, then everything
created by God will perfectly fulfil its purpose, whatever that may
be. Given that the aesthetic appreciation of an artefact involves the

---

[4] See Passmore (1980: 207).

[5] Believing that some degree of artefactualization is necessary for aesthetic appreciation, Allen Carlson (1998: iii. 348) asserts that human conceptualization and
understanding of nature is a form of artefactualization and, although minimal, is
sufficient to underwrite aesthetic appreciation of nature. But this is to misuse the
notion of the artefactual: artefactualization is not necessary for aesthetic appreciation,
and neither conceptualizing nor understanding something (a snowflake, with its
beautiful crystalline structure, say) turns it into an artefact.

appreciation of its being well or poorly designed to fulfil its purpose, those who delight aesthetically in nature as God's creation should, as far as this aspect of the appreciation of an artefact is concerned, regard everything as being satisfactory (although God's purpose might often or always be mysterious, and it might include the creation of objects intended to be aesthetically unattractive or displeasing to human beings).

Accordingly, the aesthetic appreciation of nature, as I understand the idea, if it is to be appreciation of nature *as what nature actually is*, requires not only that nature is appreciated as nature but that this appreciation does not consist in appreciating nature as an artefact. Hence—given that a work of art is an artefact—it requires that it does not essentially involve perceiving or imagining nature as a work of art. It follows that one kind of appreciation that the aesthetic appreciation of nature is opposed to is artistic appreciation, so that the appreciation of nature as art is different from the aesthetic appreciation of nature.[6] Accordingly, if an observer adopts towards nature an attitude appropriate to a work of art, regarding it as if it were such a work, the resulting experience, although aesthetic and directed at nature, falls outside the aesthetic appreciation of nature. Of course, it is possible to appreciate nature *as looking like a beautiful picture of nature*—nature as picturesque (in one sense of that expression)—although the occasions when this would be a natural thing to do are rare, since, except perhaps for landscape, nature does not in general strike us as looking like a picture—as it might when the prevailing conditions of illumination greatly weaken the impression of the third dimension—and other occasions would require the adoption of a peculiar attitude to the world, one that it does not invite. But this possibility is beside the point, for to appreciate nature as looking like a picture is not to appreciate nature as nature. In sum: the aesthetic appreciation of nature, as I understand the idea, is identical with the aesthetic appreciation not of that which is nature, but of nature *as nature and not as art (or artefact)*.

Is the aesthetic appreciation of nature confined to individuals (and individuals as related to one another) or does it extend to

---

[6] It follows that those who have assigned primacy to the aesthetic appreciation of art will find it hard to accommodate the aesthetic appreciation of nature as nature. The account of the aesthetic that I later offer assigns priority neither to the appreciation of art nor to the appreciation of nature. Of course, art can be imposed on nature, in which case aesthetic appreciation will combine the aesthetic appreciation of art with the aesthetic appreciation of nature as nature. See n. 9.

kinds? In fact, this disjunction does not exhaust the possibilities. Schopenhauer held neither of these positions but maintained, instead, that the aesthetic appreciation of nature—of the beauty of individual natural objects—is essentially the appreciation of natural kinds (understood as atemporal items), which are made manifest to us in the perception of individual instances of those kinds: we appreciate not individual natural items, nor natural kinds as realized in the specific forms of individuals, but natural kinds themselves, made available to us through the medium of the individuals we perceive. But he embraced this view in a peculiar form: natural kinds, although non-spatial and atemporal, are essentially perceptible items, object for a subject, 'representations'; in the aesthetic appreciation of nature we have an especially vivid and compelling perceptual awareness of the inner essential nature of the natural kind an individual exemplifies; and each natural kind is beautiful (Schopenhauer 1969: i. §41; 1974: ii. §212).[7] It follows from Schopenhauer's position—and he explicitly drew this conclusion (Schopenhauer 1969: i. §41)—that from the aesthetic point of view it is immaterial which instance of a natural kind is being contemplated: differences among instances are aesthetically irrelevant, since the upshot of aesthetic contemplation, which requires disregarding an item's position in space and time and so its individuality, is always the same; namely, awareness of the natural kind itself, the proper object of aesthetic contemplation. Although Schopenhauer's train of thought is not compelling, it suggests a significant difference between the aesthetic appreciation of nature and the appreciation of art: whereas two exactly similar objects of the same natural kind, two indistinguishable melons or ladybirds or sea trout, for example, must have the same aesthetic value in themselves, two exactly similar objects, as has often been pointed out, might differ in artistic meaning with a resultant difference in artistic value.[8]

---

[7] Schopenhauer's thoughts about the aesthetic appeal of natural ensembles of natural objects, rather than the aesthetic contemplation of an individual natural thing, reveal his difficulty in accommodating the insights yielded by his own aesthetic experience within the general framework of his metaphysics and aesthetics.

[8] See Walton (1970) and Danto (1983). It would, I believe, be wrong to base resistance to my conclusion on a remark by Aldo Leopold (1989: 169): 'Consider . . . a trout raised in a hatchery and newly liberated in an over-fished stream. The stream is no longer capable of natural trout production. Pollution has fouled its waters, or deforestation and trampling have warmed or silted them. No one would claim this trout has the same value as a wholly wild one caught out of some unmanaged stream in the high Rockies. Its esthetic connotations are inferior, even though its capture may require

1.3. NON-PRISTINE NATURE

Although it would be mistaken to think of nature as that part of the world that has been unchanged or not significantly affected by human agency, much of terrestrial nature has not remained in its natural condition, but has been subjected to human interference. Wild animals have been domesticated, new strains of plant developed by selective breeding, species native to one area have been transplanted to other parts of the world, rivers have been dammed, land reclaimed from the sea, hillsides terraced, seas polluted, forests felled, and so on indefinitely. In some cases, humanity's influence is detectable without specialist knowledge, being manifest in the result, at least in the short term; but often this is not so. In any case, much of our natural environment displays, for better or worse, the influence of humanity, having been shaped, to a greater or lesser extent, and in a variety of ways, by human purposes, so that little of the world's landscape is in a natural condition. If some segment of the natural environment has been affected by humanity, it can still be appreciated aesthetically as nature, but appreciation of it by one who is aware of its non-pristine character is liable to be appreciation of it as *nature affected by humanity*. Accordingly, our aesthetic experience of the natural world is often *mixed*—a mixture of the aesthetic appreciation of nature as nature with an additional element, of a variable character, based on human design or purpose or activity.[9]

skill.' Leopold is concerned with the *trophy-value* of objects such as game or fish, which is a function of the exercise of skill, persistence, or discrimination in the overcoming, outwitting, or reducing-to-possession of the trophy, the trophy-value being these connotations, which attach to the trophy, intensive management of game or fish lowering the trophy-value of the object by artificializing it. But there is no good reason to concur with Leopold's view of trophy-value as an aesthetic characteristic of the trophy: trophy-value is merely a matter of the trophy's being a reminder of what it took to capture it and the satisfaction derived from the successful exercise of one's abilities in doing so. Furthermore, even if the trophy-value of a newly liberated trout is less than that of a wholly wild one, the aesthetic value of the first to one concerned only with appreciating a trout's appearance and movements is not thereby less than that of the second—although its being there by human management might detract from the spectator's delight in coming across it.

[9] From an aesthetic point of view, the imposition of art on the natural world, or making a portion of nature into a work of art, as with garden design or the art of landscape, the aesthetic appreciation of which requires two forms of aesthetic appreciation to function hand in hand, is of special interest. There are significant differences between the appeal of 'wild' nature and any form of domesticated nature or nature stamped with human design, and within the second class there are further differences,

A scene can consist entirely of natural objects yet be constructed or planned, wholly or in part, by humanity. Accordingly, the portion of the world a spectator is appreciating, a landscape, say, might contain only natural things but include traces of humanity, in the form of orchards, fields of wheat, or pastures on which cows have been put to graze, for example. But it might contain both natural and non-natural objects, houses and bridges, for instance. In both cases, the presence and character of the non-natural element might or might not be determined by aesthetic considerations; and if partly determined by aesthetic considerations, this might be in the light of the appearance of the non-natural element from the point of view a spectator happens to occupy or the path she is following, or not so. But although a natural item is often not in its natural state or natural location or habitat, or has arisen only through human contrivance or as an intended or unintended result of human activity, or is in a scene composed of natural objects but which has not been naturally produced, or is adjacent to or surrounded by non-natural items, or has been positioned where it is not by nature but by humanity, this does not prevent it from being appreciated aesthetically as natural and does not mean that its appreciation must be mixed. For whether an item is natural is not the same as whether other aspects of the scene or other properties of the item are natural, and it is possible, with more or less difficulty in particular cases, to focus one's interest only on what is natural. Whether what you are confronted by is (entirely) natural[10] is one thing; what it is about the situation you are appreciating is another. At a zoo you cannot appreciate an animal in its natural environment. But it does not follow that your appreciation must be of a caged animal—an animal as caged. Rather, you can ignore its surroundings and appreciate the animal itself (within the severe limits imposed by its captive state). In looking at a fountain, you are not looking at a natural state of affairs. Nevertheless, you can appreciate some of the perceptible properties of water,

especially between those instances subjected to art and those not so subjected. Two excellent studies of the aesthetics of gardens are Miller (1993) and Ross (1998).

[10] If to be completely natural a scene must lack all signs of humanity, there cannot be people in it. If all that needs to be missing is signs of human artifice, then, since human bodies are natural objects, but clothed human bodies are not, although the scene cannot contain clothed human bodies it can contain naked human bodies—as long as they do not indicate artifice. (But perhaps the manifest possibility of human artifice, as indicated by the presence of human bodies, might be thought to detract from the naturalness of the scene, thus avoiding this curious result.)

a natural substance, in particular its liquidity, mobility, and the way in which it catches the light. All that follows from the fact that much of our natural environment displays the influence of humanity and that we are usually confronted by scenes that in various ways involve artifice is that the aesthetic appreciation of nature, if it is to be *pure*, must abstract from any design imposed on nature, especially a design imposed for artistic or aesthetic effect.[11]

1.4. RESPONDING TO NATURE AS NATURE

But if the aesthetic appreciation of nature is the aesthetic appreciation of nature as nature, what is meant by a 'response to nature as nature'? There are two ways in which this might be understood, which I shall call the internal and external conceptions, the first given by a strong and the other by a weak reading of the phrase, the external conception being entirely unproblematic. The weak reading understands the idea in a merely negative fashion: a response to nature as nature is just a response to nature not as whatever is opposed to nature—as art or artefact, for example (so that there is no intended meaning or function to be understood). In fact, taking nature to be opposed to art, the external conception can assume two forms, the non-artistic and the anti-artistic. The non-artistic construes 'as nature' to mean only 'not in virtue of being a work of art'. An example of the non-artistic response would be this: an observer comes across an object, does not know, and is indifferent to, whether it is a natural object or a work of art, yet finds its appearance beautiful (whatever the status of the object might be). The anti-artistic construes 'as nature' to mean 'in virtue of lacking the distinctive properties of works of art'. In this case, the observer is not indifferent to whether the object appreciated is a work of nature or of art; on the contrary, the observer's response is founded on the thought that the object is not art. The strong reading of 'response to nature as nature' requires more than the weak: a response to nature

---

[11] A beholder might not be aware that a landscape has been in some ways designed by humanity and might delight in it as nature's handiwork. In such a case, although the delight in the way in which the elements of the landscape relate to one another is aesthetic delight in what is taken to be nature as nature, it is malfounded: it is not delight in what actually is natural as being natural.

as nature is a response to nature not merely 'not as art or artefact', but 'in virtue of being natural'. Accordingly, in the case of an aesthetic response to a natural item, its being natural constitutes an element of one's appreciation, i.e. of what one appreciates, so that it grounds and enhances, diminishes, or otherwise transforms the experience. In other words: on the one hand, 'as natural' might mean 'not as designed by humanity [or another intelligent species]', so that certain possible aspects of an item—the item's being an artefact, in particular a work of art, and any characteristic of the item that being a work of art or another kind of artefact are necessary conditions of—are to be deemed *irrelevant* to its appreciation; on the other hand, 'as natural' might be understood to imply that the appreciation must be *based* on the item's being natural, in which case a replica that mimics the item's appearance, experienced as being nonnatural, would not do just as well (even if the properties that accrue to it in virtue of being an artefact are left aside). The first conception of the aesthetic appreciation of nature requires only that nature is not appreciated under a certain concept, namely that of an artefact; the second requires that nature is appreciated under a concept, namely the concept of nature itself or the concept of some particular kind of natural phenomenon.

The requirement imposed by the strong reading might induce scepticism about the possibility of the aesthetic appreciation of nature. How could an aesthetic response be founded on the fact that its object is natural? How could the fact that an item is natural be integral to, or integrated into, an aesthetic response to it? The answer is, in outline, simple. For it is a general truth that we are delighted or otherwise moved by states of affairs, processes, and so on, under certain concepts or descriptions;[12] the descriptions under which we experience something properly affect the nature of our response to it; accordingly, the fact that we experience something as natural might be integral to the emotion we feel towards it, so that if this emotion is a component of an aesthetic response to the object, this response is based on the object's being part of nature.

Consider, for example, the aesthetic appreciation of birdsong. What is the object of delight—what do we delight in—when we take an aesthetic delight in birdsong *as birdsong*? As with all other instances of the aesthetic appreciation of nature untouched by

---

[12] To experience O under description 'D' is for it to seem to you in your experience that O is D: this is how your experience represents O.

human hands, the appreciation of birdsong is free from a certain constraint of understanding, namely the understanding of its meaning as art. This is not to say that if you delight in listening to the songs of birds, your delight is aesthetic only if you hear the sounds merely as patterns of sounds. On the contrary, you hear the sounds as products of [unaided] bodily actions, of 'voices', or 'whistles', or 'warbles'. But you do not hear them as intentionally determined by artistic considerations. You delight in the seemingly endless and effortless variety of a song thrush's song—variations in pitch, timbre, dynamics, rhythm, and vocal attack, for example—but not as the product of artistry and not as a construction guided by consideration of its effectiveness as art. The song consists of a series of rhythmic phrases, the various segments differing from one another in the number of similar phrases that form the segment and in the nature of the constituent phrases, which vary in the number, duration, timbre, pitch, and loudness of the sounds that compose them. These phrases succeed one another but never seem to reach a final goal, a final ending; instead, they continue for an indefinite time in a way that does not appear to be meaningful overall. In other words, you hear the song as an unpredictable, apparently random mélange of phrases. Now the aesthetic listener is not absolutely required to ignore the actual function of the bird's singing, which is to affirm its territory and, perhaps, to attract a mate. It might even be possible to appreciate the song not just as 'music' but as especially well suited to its seductive function, although it is hard to see that any such sense of appropriateness by one of us could be securely based in an awareness of what it is like to be a female song thrush.[13] But, such a possibility aside, the song of a thrush is heard as being attractive to listen to, in its own right, in abstraction from its (possible) function of seducing the opposite sex. The object of aesthetic delight is the sounds as issuing 'naturally' from a living, sentient creature; more specifically, a bird.[14]

---

[13] We cannot even reasonably conclude how in the most fundamental sense it sounds to a song thrush on the basis of how it sounds to us. For example, a song thrush might hear additional sounds in the song, sounds too high for us to hear.

[14] But is this quite right? To appreciate it fully does one need to appreciate it as the song of *a bird*, specifically? And, if so, as the song of a particular kind of bird, a blackbird, for example? Most of us acquire, at best, the concept of a certain type of bird and, perhaps, an idea of the look of a bird of that type, or an ability to recognize such a bird by sight. Aesthetic appreciation of a bird's song appears to be the same before and after you learn which type of bird it is, or whether you know it is a song thrush, say, and how a song thrush looks, at rest or in flight.

With this illustration in mind, we can return to and fill in the outline answer to the sceptical doubt. In one sense, what you experience when you experience an item under one description is not the same as what you experience if you experience that item under another, incompatible, description. In other words, your experience of an item is sensitive to what you experience it as, so that an experience of it under one description has a different phenomenology from that of an experience under an incompatible description. Furthermore, the description under which you experience something constrains the qualities that such an item can manifest to you, that is, that it can display as an item of the kind that falls under that description; and so qualities of an item available under one description might not be available under another description. It follows that there is no difficulty in the idea of a response to nature being a response to it *as* nature. Hence, scepticism about the idea of the aesthetic appreciation of nature must be focused specifically on the possibility of an *aesthetic* response to nature as nature. But how easy or difficult it is for nature, or a particular natural item, to meet the requirement imposed by the internal conception turns on the idea of the aesthetic, more specifically, the idea of an aesthetic response to something. It is therefore necessary to clarify the idea of an aesthetic response.

1.5. THE CHARACTER OF AN AESTHETIC RESPONSE

What makes a response *aesthetic*? Is it the intrinsic nature of the response or the nature of the features to which it is a response? What constitutes aesthetic, as opposed to non-aesthetic, appreciation? What is necessary, and what is sufficient, for a response to something to be an aesthetic response to that item?

Many attempts have been made to capture the notion of what is aesthetic, concentrating on the idea of aesthetic judgement, or the idea of aesthetic properties, or the idea of the aesthetic attitude, aesthetic experience, pleasure, or emotion, or some other aspect of the aesthetic. But whatever their merits such attempts do not command assent, if they are seen as attempts to capture some commonly and pre-theoretically recognized notion of the aesthetic. For the idea of the aesthetic, as it occurs in everyday speech, is too indefinite to merit close attention, and its use in philosophy is multivalued and liable to be driven by theory. This is apparent in the problematic scope of the aesthetic. For there are different conceptions of its scope. For example, it could be used, as it is by some aestheticians, in a wide sense to include the idea of artistic appreciation, representing artistic appreciation as the aesthetic appreciation of works of art. But some prefer a narrower sense according to which, although aesthetic experience—an experience of, for example, beauty, repose, liveliness, unity, expressiveness—is elicited by works of art, non-artistic artefacts, and nature, artistic appreciation is not primarily a matter of aesthetic experience: works of art are not primarily aesthetic objects, objects created with the intention of providing rewarding aesthetic experiences, and, moreover, there can be non-aesthetic art. And, clearly, this point of view, which insists on a distinction between aesthetic properties of works of art (gracefulness, say) and artistic properties (such as originality) and between a work's aesthetic and its artistic value, operates with a narrower sense of 'aesthetic'. But this divergence in understanding is not the only one. For some distinguish aesthetic pleasure from purely sensory (or sensuous) pleasure, such as delight in a colour or taste, whereas others think of purely sensory pleasure as being a species of aesthetic pleasure. Some require aesthetic pleasure to be pleasure in (perceptual) structure—in this way distinguishing it from 'purely sensory' pleasure. Others insist that pleasure is aesthetic only if it involves the exercise of conceptual powers—in this different way distinguishing it from the 'purely sensory'. Some deny that all forms of artistic appreciation are aesthetic, allowing into the aesthetic only those arts that address a specific sensory mode (or a number of such modes), thus placing the appreciation of literature outside the aesthetic. And so on.

This means that the boundaries of the aesthetic are uncertain and a definition of what is aesthetic cannot be tested by determining whether it picks out all and only those judgements, responses, interests, attitudes, forms of appreciation (or whatever) that fall within these boundaries. The best that can be hoped for, therefore, is an account that imposes discipline on our use of the concept by capturing what, once articulated, appears to be central to at least one familiar conception of the idea; that is neutral about the relative importance or priority of art and nature within the field of the aesthetic; and that chimes with our own experience of nature, art, and other objects of aesthetic interest.

An attractive conception of the aesthetic along the required lines is, I suggest, this: a response is aesthetic in so far as the response is directed at the experienced properties of an item, the nature and arrangement of its elements or the interrelationships among its parts or aspects, and it involves a positive or negative reaction to the item not as satisfying a desire for the existence or non-existence of some state of affairs in which the item figures, but considered 'in itself' (in abstraction from any personal relation that might obtain between subject and object), so that what governs the response is whether the object is intrinsically rewarding or displeasing to experience in itself. 'An item' includes not just physical objects or combinations of objects, but also the activity or behaviour of living or non-living things, events or processes of other kinds, mere appearances, and any other kind of thing that is susceptible of aesthetic appreciation. By 'experienced properties' I mean properties the item is experienced as possessing, in perception, thought, or imagination, and the notion is to be understood in an all-embracing sense, covering not only immediately perceptible properties, but also relational, representational, symbolic, and emotional properties as they are realized in the item, and including the kind or type of thing the item is experienced as being. By a positive reaction I mean a reaction of attraction to the item, one that involves the disposition to continue to attend to it; by a negative reaction I mean the converse. (I allow the possibility of a mixed response, of fascinated horror, for example, or the double-aspect experience of the sublime.)[15] Given Kant's conception of pleasure, such reactions would be experiences of pleasure and displeasure, respectively. For although Kant regarded pleasure as being indefinable, he held that it is integral to a representation's being pleasant that it has a causality inherent in it that tends to preserve the continuation of the state. If, as I believe, he held the converse as well, his notion of an experience of pleasure is much the same as that of an experience that is inherently rewarding. But it is not essential to

---

[15] An evaluative aesthetic judgement—one that evaluates an item aesthetically—attributes some degree of aesthetic value, positive, negative, *or zero*. In accordance with this, the idea of an aesthetic response could be adjusted so as to include one of *indifference*. Alternatively, an evaluative aesthetic judgement that attributes zero degree of aesthetic value might be thought of as one expressive of the fact that the subject has no aesthetic response to the item judged, which would require no adjustment. The choice between these alternatives is of no importance.

my conception of an aesthetic response that these reactions should be thought of as forms of pleasure or displeasure. On a narrower conception of pleasure than Kant's, although a positive reaction might well be an experience of pleasure, it would not necessarily be so. What is essential to a positive reaction is that the subject should find the object to be in some way inherently rewarding to experience. The condition that the positive or negative reaction should not be the satisfaction of a desire for the existence or non-existence of some state of affairs in which the object of the response figures—a condition that an aesthetic response must, on my understanding of the notion, satisfy—is needed to ensure that aesthetic pleasure [or displeasure] is 'disinterested' in Kant's sense. For a pleasure not to be an interest—to be disinterested—is for it not to be a *propositional* pleasure, pleasure in *a fact*, and this implies that the pleasure is not the satisfaction of one of the subject's desires that the world should be a certain way. No propositional pleasure is an aesthetic pleasure.

Such a conception of an aesthetic response applies to nature and art; it allows for the aesthetic appreciation of sport, juggling, circus acts, furniture, clothes, wine, motor cars, machines, tools of all kinds, and much else; it does not discriminate against certain kinds of perceptible property in favour of one privileged kind; and it does not restrict aesthetic experience to a small class of categories (such as experiences of the beautiful and the sublime).[16] For the present purpose it does not matter if this conception is thought not to exhaust the nature of an aesthetic response, or to be inferior to some alternative conception, as long as the satisfaction of the condition it articulates is considered sufficient for a response reasonably to be deemed aesthetic.

1.6.   AN AESTHETIC RESPONSE TO NATURE AS NATURE

We now have an understanding of the idea of (the internal conception of) a response to nature as nature, and also the idea of an

[16] Traditionally, the aesthetic appreciation of nature was often thought of as consisting of two (positive) kinds: the aesthetic experience of the beautiful and the aesthetic experience of the sublime. How comprehensive this typology is, and in particular whether it is exhaustive of the possibilities, depends on how these two kinds of experience are characterized. It will not be exhaustive unless the beautiful covers all purely positive possible aesthetic responses to nature, and the sublime all positive responses with an admixture of negative emotion.

aesthetic response. If we marry these two ideas we have the idea of
an aesthetic response to nature as nature. What this comes to is, in
effect, the idea of a response to a natural item, grounded on its
naturalness—on its being a part of nature or on its being a specific
kind of natural item—focused on its elements or aspects as structured or interrelated in the item, the item being experienced as
intrinsically rewarding, unrewarding, or displeasing, the hedonic
character of the reaction being 'disinterested'. So the question is
whether—and, if so, how—nature, or a particular natural item,
can be the intentional object of such a response. In what way, if
any, can the fact that something is natural, or a certain kind of
natural thing, ground an aesthetic response to it?

How the very naturalness of an object—the mere fact that the
object is natural, not its being a natural thing of a certain kind—can
properly ground an aesthetic response to it is severely limited,[17] for
what is common to all natural items in virtue of being natural is only
a negative, not a positive, characteristic: they must not be the products of human skill or design or artifice. This leaves only such a
possibility as marvelling at the fact that something as beautiful,
attractive, or remarkable as *this*—a rainbow or the exquisite fan-
shaped leaf of a ginkgo, for example—is a product of nature. So if
the idea of the aesthetic appreciation of nature as nature (on the
internal conception) is coherent and the aesthetic appreciation of
nature can have a more substantial foundation than the mere naturalness of its object, there must be aspects or properties that a natural
item can possess in virtue of which it can be appreciated aesthetically
as natural. What kinds of feature might these be?

Now nature exhibits a remarkable variety of very different kinds
of thing—living and non-living, sentient and non-sentient, animal
and non-animal, and so on—and the aesthetic appreciation of
nature ranges over everything in nature,[18] often in more than one

[17] Compare and contrast the difficulty in seeing how the mere fact that an item is a
work of art—rather than some specific property it possesses in virtue of being
not nature but a work of art—could ground an aesthetic response to the item *as*
a work of art.
[18] The aesthetic appreciation of nature is often restricted to the 'macroscopic'. But
there is no good reason for excluding microscopic entities or the appearances of
natural items (snowflakes, for example) when seen not with the naked eye but under
a microscope. There is no relevant difference between unaided perception, perception
by means of a microscope, and many other forms of aided perception— perception of
distant objects by optical telescopes, for example.

way, involving either a single perceptual mode or a combination, focusing on a single natural object, at rest or in motion, at
a moment or over time, or a product of a natural object, or a
complex of natural items, or a natural process, or an appearance
or impression (perhaps a changing one, as when mist slowly clears
or the sun rises or sets). It would therefore be exceptionally daunt-
ing and probably fruitless to attempt an exhaustive account of the
kinds of aspects in virtue of which natural items can be appreciated
aesthetically *as* natural. But the principle that would underlie
such an attempt is clear. The crucial question is: what qualities
capable of aesthetic appreciation—in themselves or in virtue of
their contribution to an overall aesthetic effect or structure—might
be possessed by an item in virtue of being natural or in virtue
of being a certain kind of natural item? So what is required is the
identification of characteristics that are capable of figuring in aesthetic appreciation, whether this is positive or negative, and
that accrue to an item only in virtue of its being a natural item of a
certain kind.

It is easy to indicate examples of such characteristics. For
instance, there are qualities that can accrue to something only
because it is a form of life. A living thing has a history of a distinctive
kind, a life of growth and decline, nourished by its environment, at
the mercy of the elements, perhaps responding to or anticipating
changes in the seasons, its external appearance being determined by
natural processes and structures within it; and this enables its condition at a certain time to be seen as a stage in or phase of its
development, wherein it is flourishing or wilting, in a state of need
or decay, and as contrasting with earlier or later conditions. Thus
the fact that a natural item is a tree allows its form to be seen as
determined by its internal nature, its age, its habitat, and the friendly
or hostile forces of nature, and its condition at any time of the year
to be seen as determined by the cycle of the seasons. This enables the
aesthetic observer to delight not only in the visual appearance of its
blossoms, say, but in what they indicate, and to experience the
flowering of the tree as a manifestation and beautiful expression of
the resurgence of life triggered by the arrival of spring; or to marvel
at the way in which the tree, restricted by its intrinsic nature, has
adjusted to the constraints imposed on it by its location, its environment, and the climate. Again, there are many kinds of quality that
accrue to an item only in virtue of its being a sentient thing, capable

of locomotion. For example, only sentient creatures can be seen as looking at or otherwise perceiving the world, and in particular as being aware of the presence of another creature, and so as exploring, hunting, diving, disputing a territory, or engaging in courtship rituals; and there are styles of movement that are specific to sentient creatures, as with the graceful movements of a gazelle, and styles of movement that only sentient creatures of a certain kind are capable of, as with the various forms of the flight of birds. These open the possibility of a distinctive kind of aesthetic delight—at the cavorting of an otter or a school of dolphins at play or the exploratory behaviour of a fox cub or the outstanding aerial manoeuvrability of dragonflies (enhanced by their gossamer, jewel-like wings and brightly-coloured bodies), for instance. Furthermore, the parts of both sentient and insentient living things, animals and plants, for example, have natural functions, and a sentient creature has a style of life determined by its nature. In each kind of case, there is a possible source of aesthetic delight focused on the idea of suitability: the parts of these living things can be seen as manifestly or strikingly suitable to discharging their functions, especially in the given environment and climate, and the creature can be seen as perfectly suited to its style of life. As David Hume (1961: §VI, pt. II) wrote: 'It is evident, that one considerable source of *beauty* in all animals is the advantage which they reap from the particular structure of their limbs and members, suitably to the particular manner of life, to which they are by nature destined'—as with 'the structure . . . of the woodpecker, with its feet, tail, beak, and tongue, so admirably adapted to catch insects under the bark of trees' (Darwin 1929: 2). The well-known opening lines of Hopkins's 'The Windhover', which seek to capture a falcon's manner of flight and an observer's emotional response to the enviable ability that enables the falcon to flourish in the element in which it must live, provide a vivid illustration:

> I caught this morning morning's minion, king-
>> dom of daylight's dauphin, dapple-dawn-drawn Falcon, in his riding
>> Of the rolling level underneath him steady air, and striding
> High there, how he rung upon the rein of a wimpling wing
> In his ecstasy! then off, off forth on swing,
>> As a skate's heel sweeps smooth on a bow-bend: the hurl and gliding
>> Rebuffed the big wind. My heart in hiding
> Stirred for a bird,—the achieve of, the mastery of the thing!

As these examples show, there is no inherent difficulty in the concept of the aesthetic appreciation of nature: whichever conception of a response to nature as nature is preferred, the idea of the aesthetic appreciation of nature as nature is coherent and it is possible for the aesthetic appreciation of nature to be solidly founded on characteristics that accrue to items in virtue of their being natural items of certain kinds.

1.7.   KNOWLEDGE OF NATURE

A further clarification of the idea of the aesthetic appreciation of nature is achieved by the resolution of a number of interlinked issues about the identification of natural things, ignorance of their nature, mistakes about them, and the relevance of 'scientific' understanding. What kind of understanding of nature does a correct and full aesthetic appreciation of it require? Do we need the knowledge of the natural scientist—the naturalist, the geologist, the biologist, and the ecologist?[19] Does experiencing something with 'scientific' understanding of it deepen or enhance the aesthetic appreciation of it? Does it matter aesthetically whether you correctly experience something as being a certain type of natural phenomenon or of natural kind K? Does it matter whether you mis-experience something as being of a certain natural kind?[20] Does it matter whether you are not mistaken about but ignorant of the natural kind you are appreciating?[21]

Clearly, the mere ability to identify things as being of certain types on the basis of their appearance, to classify them (either under 'everyday' or 'technical' categories), to give names to them—to

[19] As Allen Carlson has argued: see, for example, Carlson (1979*a*).

[20] The question concerns the misidentification of the natural kind to which the object belongs, not the misidentification of a natural object as a work of art or vice versa. This other question (along with much else, especially significant differences between the aesthetic appreciation of nature and artistic appreciation, about which I have said nothing in this essay) is well dealt with in Hepburn's seminal (1966). There are further kinds of misunderstanding of the natural world that affect the aesthetic appreciation of nature, but these are also not my concern here.

[21] Ignorance about the natural kind you are appreciating can be more or less extreme: you might see a flower but not as a flower, only as a coloured three-dimensional natural object of some kind jutting from the earth; or you might see an arum lily as a flower of some kind, but one that you do not recognize.

clouds, for example—does not thereby endow the subject with an enhanced appreciation of nature, although it may be the result of or encourage or facilitate a heightened or finer or richer awareness of natural features.[22] But there are cases where knowledge of the nature of a phenomenon—not merely the ability to identify that type—can transform one's aesthetic experience of nature. People have thicker or thinner conceptions of the nature of the phenomena which they see or otherwise perceive under concepts of those phenomena: children have exceptionally thin conceptions, adults have conceptions of greater and varying thickness. The thicker the conception, the greater the material available to transform the subject's aesthetic experience of nature. It follows that people can recruit to their perceptions of natural phenomena different levels of understanding, superficial or deep. If you have the right kind of understanding of nature, you can recruit to your perceptual experience of nature relevant thoughts, emotions, and images unavailable to those who lack that understanding—as when you see a 'shooting star' *as* the glow of a meteor burning in the earth's atmosphere, or a gigantic crater *as* having been produced by the impact of a meteorite, or a canyon *as* having been cut by a swift-flowing river, or a mountain *as* a massive block of rock thrust up by enormous pressures beneath the earth's surface, or—an extreme case—the Himalayas *as* the product of a collision between the Indian subcontinent and the main bulk of Asia, or obsidian *as* a coal-black volcanic glass composed of fast-cooled lava, or stalactites, stalagmites, and helictites *as* formed by minerals deposited by dripping water, or broomrape *as* a parasite that feeds on other plants. And the transformation your experience undergoes when relevant knowledge is enlisted carries with it the possibility of varieties of aesthetic appreciation of nature and species of aesthetic emotional responses otherwise unavailable.[23]

Consider the aesthetic appreciation of clouds or sky-scapes. Just as lightning is not merely an optical (and acoustical) phenomenon, but a violent, sometimes dangerous, discharge of electricity, so

---

[22] But unless you see O as being of natural kind K, you cannot experience it as being, or not being, an especially beautiful specimen *of that kind*.

[23] The transformation of perception effected by knowledge of the nature of an object of aesthetic appreciation will by no means always result in an intensification of aesthetic delight. On the contrary, it can diminish or erase it, as might happen when a plant is seen as poisonous; or the beautiful appearance of a turquoise sea anemone might recede or disappear when its protuberances are seen as tentacles with the power to paralyse small prey and its greenish centre is seen as its mouth.

clouds are not merely optical phenomena, but aggregations of microscopic droplets of water suspended in the atmosphere. Their two- or three-dimensional apparent shapes and their colouration may be and often are beautiful, but their aesthetic appreciation is not confined to these directly visible aspects. For, given that clouds are three-dimensional masses, composed of minute droplets of water, formed by, at the mercy of, and bringing about processes in the atmosphere, that they float, are at rest, meet, are being torn apart or expanding rapidly, and so on, they possess more aspects open to aesthetic appreciation than their shapes and colours. The transformations in the sky's appearance brought about by changes in the clouds, which at times enact spectacular dramas, are seen by the informed watcher as the expression of various natural forces at work in the atmosphere and are appreciated aesthetically as such. If when looking at a cloud you identify its type as cumulonimbus, your aesthetic experience is not thereby transformed. But if, in virtue of additional knowledge, you see the anvil top and ragged base of a cumulonimbus as a *thunder cloud*, your impression of the cloud might change, for you might now have a sense of *power* in the cloud and see it *as* shaped by powerful forces at work in it; and this sense of power will inform your experience and change the nature of your aesthetic response.[24] Or consider the experience of looking at the Milky Way. As a child, you might experience it just as a white streak with a somewhat milky appearance running across the night sky. You might then come to see it as being the appearance of an exceptional congregation of stars in that region of the night sky, but possess no greater understanding of it. Finally, when you realize the truth about what you are seeing and why you are seeing it, your experience can assume quite a different nature: you now experience the Milky Way as the view into the heart of our galaxy, and by the use of your imagination you 'see' yourself as located on a small planet of a minor star on one of the spiralling arms near the edge of the galaxy into whose heart you are looking. A correct under-standing of what is visible in the night sky thus makes possible a transformation of your experience from a condition in which you are struck by a milky path running across the sky to one in which your

---

[24] This is a prime example of what Hepburn (1966) calls 'realizing'—making vivid to perception or imagination the nature of an object of perception (the tremendous height and inner turbulence of a cumulonimbus cloud, for example). He rightly identifies this as one of the chief activities in the aesthetic appreciation of nature.

position in the universe—your position and that of everyone else you care about—is manifest to you in a manner that encourages an awareness of the minute stage on which the history of humanity unfolds, the peripheral status of what happens on the earth even in our own galaxy, the awesome immensity of the multitude of stars that compose that galaxy, and the realization that you are forever isolated from whatever civilizations, perhaps countlessly many, are present elsewhere in space and that you must remain ignorant of their different natures and histories, no matter how fascinating these might be. Such thoughts, harnessed to your perceptual experience, constitute an important change in your perspective, and are likely to produce one of those peculiar combinations of mental states that have been called experiences of the sublime—in this case a feeling of wonder combined with an experience of vulnerability woven together with a sense of the relative insignificance of your individual self, a mental state with both a positive and a negative side, a duality that has often been thought of as the hallmark of an experience of the sublime.[25]

But this is not to say that knowledge of the nature of a phenomenon always endows the subject with the ability to transform her perception of the world and facilitate an enhancement of aesthetic appreciation. Many of us know the explanation of rainbows, but not so many of us know the explanation of supernumerary bows. In either case, it seems that possession of the explanation does not make possible an aesthetic experience of its object that is otherwise unavailable. Most of us know that water is H_2O, but this knowledge does not enable an enhanced aesthetic appreciation of water, in dew, mist, rain, snow, rivers, or waterfalls, for example. For knowledge of the nature of a natural phenomenon to be able to effect a transformation of the subject's aesthetic experience of it, the knowledge must be such that it can permeate or inform the perception of the phenomenon, so that what the subject sees it *as* is different from how it is seen by someone who lacks the requisite knowledge. We do not see water or copper differently from one who is ignorant of their nature: we do not see water as H_2O or copper as possessing atomic number 29, for the knowledge we bring to our perception is not such as to integrate with the perception in such a manner as to generate a new perceptual-cum-imaginative content of experience.

[25] See Essay 2, III, §17.

If you mis-experience an item as being of natural kind K through misperception, then of course your aesthetic appreciation of it is malfounded. But to mis-experience an item as being of a certain natural kind is not of any aesthetic significance if, first, there's no error in perception, and, second, the mistake is merely a matter of getting the *name* wrong, as when I can see a flower perfectly clearly, mistakenly take it to be an orchid (when in fact it is a fritillary) and have no further knowledge of or belief about either kind. Suppose, however, that you do have some relevant knowledge of two natural kinds and you misidentify the natural kind to which an item belongs, the mistake not being founded on misperception. In such a case, the item will usually possess many aspects that you can respond to aesthetically without error *as* aspects of a natural thing, although you are mistaken about what kind of thing it is.[26] But if you aesthetically appreciate a natural object as an instance of natural kind K and it is not of kind K, then your appreciation is, in that respect, malfounded, and an awareness of your mistake undermines *that* aspect of your appreciation. For it is no longer available to you with respect to that object and you must reject as mistaken the enjoyment or excitement you felt that arose from that misapprehension. Furthermore, your misidentification might in any case result in aesthetic deprivation, for the correct identification of the type of natural object before you might enable an additional element of aesthetic appreciation of nature as nature: perceiving the thing under its true kind might allow not only the appreciation of all that the mistaken identification allows that is not malfounded, but something aesthetically valuable in addition.

[26] As Noël Carroll (1993) has emphasized, and has illustrated with someone's taking a whale to be a fish, rather than a mammal.

2

Kant's Aesthetics of Nature

I. Kant on Natural Beauty

I see the wild flowers, in their summer morn
Of beauty, feeding on joy's luscious hours;
The gay convolvulus, wreathing round the thorn,
Agape for honey showers;
And slender kingcup, burnished with the dew
Of morning's early hours,
Like gold yminted new...

John Clare, 'Summer Images'

2.1. INTRODUCTION

A theory of the aesthetic appreciation of nature will be well founded
only if it is based on a conception of what it is for appreciation to be
aesthetic. If appreciation is understood as consisting in or at least as
being informed by correct or sound valuation, aesthetic appreciation
is or is permeated by well-grounded aesthetic valuation, which
implies that the basis of a well-founded theory of the aesthetic appreciation of nature will be a conception of what it is for a judgement to
be aesthetic. Kant's theory is the most perfect realization of this
ideal: his conception of an aesthetic judgement is the theory's foundation; and the classification offered by the theory of different types
of aesthetic judgement about natural items is extracted from
this conception through reflection on the character of nature. This
classification, although somewhat marred by the acceptance of a
philosophically conventional taxonomy and, accordingly, incom-
plete, is, I believe, unsurpassed in the sureness with which basic
distinctions are drawn and the various similarities and differences
amongst kinds of aesthetic judgement are indicated. Kant's theory is

further distinguished by its concern to identify the nature of the pleasures underlying or associated with aesthetic judgements about nature—what exactly these pleasures are pleasures in and what psychological processes or mechanisms give rise to them—and by its articulation and attempted vindication of claims that might be made for these pleasures. But his analyses of the various kinds of aesthetic judgement about natural items and identification of the pleasures on which they are founded are, I believe, not always correct. Furthermore, he fails to establish more than one of the claims he makes about the kinds of pleasure involved in the appreciation of nature. Nevertheless, a firm grasp of the virtues of Kant's theory, which display themselves in an adequate presentation of it, and a realization of its defects, which need to be demonstrated, yield a more profound insight into the aesthetic appreciation of nature than is afforded by any other theory.

2.2. KANT'S NOTION OF AN AESTHETIC JUDGEMENT

For Kant, an aesthetic judgement is a judgement whose 'determining ground' cannot be other than 'subjective', which means that its determining ground cannot be other than the feeling of pleasure or displeasure (*CJ*, §1).[1] What Kant has in mind by an aesthetic judgement is a judgement made about something on the basis of experiencing that thing. His idea is that the nature of your experience of an object provides you with a reason to make a positive or negative aesthetic judgement about the object only if you react to the perception of the object with pleasure or displeasure—your judgement requires this as its ground. In other words, your judgement of something you are experiencing is aesthetic only if your judgement is of such a kind that it must be determined by the pleasurable or

---

[1] References to Immanuel Kant, *Critique of Judgement* (= *CJ*) are by section number and/or the pagination in volume v of the standard Prussian Academy edition of Kant's works. I have consulted the four English translations of the work, by J. H. Bernard, J. C. Meredith, Werner S. Pluhar, and Paul Guyer and Eric Matthews, the last three of which include the pagination of the Prussian Academy edition. The last two contain the *First Introduction to the Critique of Judgement* (= *FI*). References to Kant's *Critique of Pure Reason* (= *CPR*) are, as is standard, by the page numbers of the first (A) and second (B) editions.

unpleasurable nature of your experience of it, so that you would lack any reason to make that judgement on the basis of your experience of the item if you were not to experience it with pleasure or displeasure. This implies that an aesthetic judgement concerns an item's capacity or suitability to provide pleasure or displeasure to someone who experiences it, either to the subject alone or to some wider class—to all adult human beings with normal perceptual capacities, to those with an undeformed human nature, to those who satisfy certain requirements of knowledge, experience, and imagination, to those with a feeling for morality, or whatever. For if the content of an aesthetic judgement did not involve a reference to pleasure or displeasure, it would not be necessary that its determining ground should be the subject's pleasure or displeasure in experiencing the object of the judgement: it is just because an aesthetic judgement asserts the capacity or suitability of an object to give pleasure or displeasure that, given that it must be based on the nature of the subject's experience of the object (independently of other information), the judging subject's experience of pleasure or displeasure must play the crucial role Kant's theory assigns to it.

2.3.   KANT'S CLASSIFICATION OF (NON-COMPOUND) AESTHETIC JUDGEMENTS

In accordance with this conception of an aesthetic judgement, Kant distinguishes three non-compound kinds of aesthetic judgement, two of them being so-called reflective judgements.[2] By calling them non-compound I mean that judgements of these three kinds consist neither of a combination of aesthetic judgements nor of an aesthetic judgement combined with a non-aesthetic judgement. Each such judgement *concerns the merely material nature of an object or array of objects as this is apparent in perception*, this nature being considered independently of what kind or kinds of object they are. These judgements are *not based on concepts* of the kinds of things being judged or evaluated: such a judgement about an object does not take into account what kind of object this is an instance of. Now a material object is formed matter: matter that has a boundary, or

---

[2] For Kant's idea of a reflective judgement see Budd (2001*b*).

set of boundaries, however indefinite. Kant identifies, first, an aesthetic judgement about an object's *form*—a judgement about the pleasantness of its boundary or the set of boundaries of its parts—a *pure* judgement of taste, the judgement of *'free'* beauty.[3] Kant conceives of all pure judgements of taste as being singular judgements. A generalization such as 'Roses in general are beautiful' or a universal judgement such as 'All tulips are beautiful' is, he maintains, not a purely aesthetic judgement but a logical judgement founded on an aesthetic judgement (*CJ*, §§8, 33). Of course, since some tulips are ill-formed, wilting, or attacked by disease, the universal judgement that all tulips are beautiful would need some qualification to be at all plausible; and, since not all well-developed, flourishing tulips have the same form, and small differences in form can affect beauty of form, even the qualified claim would be exceptionally hazardous. Second, he identifies an aesthetic judgement about the perceptual appearance of any constituent[4] of an object's *matter*—a judgement about the pleasantness of a colour, taste, smell, or sound—the judgement of what is *agreeable*. Finally, he identifies an aesthetic judgement that is concerned with neither the character of the matter nor that of the form of an object but, instead, is about *boundlessness*, boundlessness in extent or power, in or at least occasioned by the matter of the object a subject is faced with—a judgement about the object's suitability to arouse the feeling of the subject's possession of a quality superior to any of mere sensibility, however immense, and in particular to the immensity of what he or she is now confronted by—another pure aesthetic judgement, the judgement of the *sublime* (in nature). Kant maintains that whilst it is not built into a judgement of the agreeable that it claims to be universally valid for human beings—and no such claim on its behalf would be warranted—a claim to universal validity is intrinsic to both judgements of the beautiful and judgements of the sublime; and for that reason, unlike the beautiful and the sublime, Kant assigns no substantial value to the agreeable and has no real interest in it. But, although judgements of the beautiful and of the sublime are alike in

---

[3] An impure judgement of taste is a judgement that combines beauty with either the agreeable or a concept.

[4] Or, perhaps—there is some uncertainty in Kant's position—a number of such elements, considered independently of their relations to one another. (Kant's notion of form, as defined in the first *Critique*, is 'that which so determines the manifold of appearance that it allows of being ordered in certain relations' (*CPR*, A20/B34).)

claiming universal validity, whereas a judgement of the beautiful stands in need of a 'deduction', the establishment of its credentials as a bona fide judgement with a non-relative truth-value, or the rightfulness of its demand for universal agreement, a deduction that Kant attempts to provide, Kant claims that the 'exposition' of a judgement of the sublime makes any further deduction of its credentials redundant.

Each of these kinds of aesthetic judgement can be about, or immediately occasioned by, either a natural object (or array of natural objects) or a product of human artifice.[5] But if the judgement is directed towards what is in fact a natural object, it is not integral to the judgement, or the hedonic state on which it is founded, that the object is, or is experienced as, or as if it were, natural, *a fortiori*, a natural object of whatever kind it happens or appears to be: the judgement of a natural colour or the colour of a natural object or a naturally produced sound or the taste or smell of a natural substance as being agreeable, the judgement of a natural object's form as being beautiful, the judgement of a natural array or phenomenon as being sublime—none of these is a judgement of its object as being natural. A pure judgement of taste, a judgement of free beauty, will be a judgement about something that is of a certain kind, K, but it will not be a judgement of it *as being* of that kind. If you see the object as being of kind K, you might express your pure judgement of taste in the form 'This K is beautiful'. But this, as the expression of a pure judgement of taste, is really a conjunction of judgements, namely 'This is a K' and 'This is beautiful', the second of which is a judgement of free beauty. So the content of your judgement of free beauty is exactly the same as that made by someone who is unaware that the object is of that kind and who expresses her judgement in the form 'This—whatever it is—is beautiful'. A judgement of free beauty about a flower, say, will be a judgement *of* the flower that it is beautiful, not a judgement that it is a beautiful flower, or a beautiful morning glory flower (if that is what it is recognized as being): it will be a judgement about what in fact is a flower, but not a judgement of it as being a flower or a flower of a certain type. Likewise, a judgement of the sublime provoked by the

---

[5] Although Kant insists that there is an impropriety in not judging a work of fine art under the concept of a work of art, i.e. as a work of art: a work of fine art must be recognized to be art, not nature (*CJ*, §45, 306); and a judgement of artistic beauty is an assessment of a work as a work of art (*CJ*, §48, 311).

star-studded night sky now visible overhead will be a judgement *of* it, but not as being the natural phenomenon it is or is perceived to be. Accordingly, although an aesthetic judgement of any one of these kinds about nature is a form of aesthetic appreciation of nature—of something that is in fact natural—it does not constitute aesthetic appreciation of nature as nature.[6]

2.4. THE DISTINCTIVE PLEASURE OF THE BEAUTIFUL

When Kant asserts that a pure judgement of taste is not based on a [determinate][7] concept, he means that the distinctive pleasure of the beautiful, the pleasure in an object that is the basis, or is constitutive, of the object's being experienced as beautiful, the pleasure in it as being beautiful, is not in any way due to the object's being experienced as falling under a concept, to the object's being experienced as being an instance of an empirical kind. The fact that in a pure judgement of taste pleasure in a beautiful natural object is not based on a concept of the natural kind the object instantiates does not require—what some take Kant's view to be—that the object must be experienced but without its being experienced as falling under a concept (of that natural kind): all it requires is that the judging subject abstracts from any empirical concept under which the subject perceives the object. Although Kant often writes as though his conception of a pure judgement of taste requires the subject to experience an object without conceptualizing it as being an instance of some kind—a requirement that would render his conception nugatory—he is aware that it does not: 'A judgement of taste about an object with a definite intrinsic purpose would be pure only if the person judging either had no concept of this purpose or abstracted from it in making his judgement' (*CJ*, §16, 231). Since the judgement concerns only the object's 'form', and Kant conceives of the perceptual form of an object as covering only spatio-temporal

[6] At least, it does not constitute aesthetic appreciation of nature as nature in the positive sense of that idea. See Essay 1, §4.

[7] A determinate (determinable) concept is a concept that is (can be) exemplified in experience. In his resolution of the Antinomy of Taste Kant maintains that a pure judgement of taste *is* based on a concept, but one that is indeterminable (*CJ*, §57).

relations amongst elements or parts of the object (*CJ*, §14, 225–6),[8] the pleasure (in the unchanging appearance of a spatial object) arises only from the perceived spatial structure of the object's matter, the spatial relations perceived to obtain among its elements, the way in which its matter is distributed across the space segment it occupies, the form of the sensory appearance of the object considered in abstraction from any concepts it falls under.

Kant's identification of the distinctive pleasure of the beautiful invokes his distinction between (passive) sensibility and (active) understanding, the sensuous as opposed to the intellectual, what is 'given' in perception as opposed to what is 'thought', the first constituting an 'immediate' relation with the object in its singularity, the second relating to the object 'mediately' through a universal characteristic, one that a number of objects may have in common. In what follows, I do not question this distinction. In fact, some form of the distinction is, I believe, essential, as the difference between perception and mere thought suggests. For perception presents its basic content in a different manner from thought: the mode of presentation—the manner in which what is represented *is* represented—in [mere] thought is different from that in perception, which presents its content sensuously (by means of sensibility, as Kant would say). Whether or not Kant countenanced the possibility of an object's being 'given' in perception without being in any way 'thought' by the subject,[9] as he seems to do,[10] it is clear that for Kant the conceptual content of a perception is only part of its representational content. Consider the example provided by the *Jäsche Logic* (Kant 1992: 544–5): a 'savage' who sees a distant house, the use of which he does not know, and another person who sees the house and knows it to be a building in which humans dwell differ, according to Kant, in that whereas the

---

[8] Kant's conception of form, which excludes the 'variety and contrast' of colours, for example, is restrictive, and unnecessarily so. It is restrictive because if the perceptual form of an object is the structure of its perceptible elements, then relations among colours are just as much part of an object's perceptual form as are its outer shape and inner contours. It is unnecessarily so because it is not necessary to exclude relations among colours in order to effect a deduction of pure judgements of taste along Kantian lines.

[9] I am inclined to believe that Kant conceived of the perceptual states of non-human animals in this fashion: they perceive the world, thus enabling them to react differentially to surrounding objects, but without their perceptions constituting *judgements*. A passage in *CPR*, A546–7/B574–5 seems to imply that non-human animals, although they possess sensibility, lack understanding.

[10] At, for example, *CPR*, A89–91/B122–3.

'cognition' of the former is mere intuition, that of the latter is both intuition and concept. Whether this is the correct account of the difference between the two perceptions, whether the representational content of a perceptual experience can be partly or wholly non-conceptual, and whether perceptual representation is through and through conceptual or is founded on non-conceptual representation or possesses a non-conceptual dimension[11] are questions that can be left aside. For it is clear that there is a sense in which the representational content of the two perceptions might be alike in every respect except that the one has an additional content determined by a concept present in it but absent from the other; that the difference in the contents consists in the concept of a dwelling under which one person, but not the other, sees the house; and that the content of each perception is, partly or wholly, determined by a component defined by analogue elements, such as colour, shape, size, direction, and distance, which component the perception acquires in virtue of an aspect of the experience different in kind from one that involves or imports such a concept as that of a dwelling, even if this component is not properly thought of as being non-conceptual. Kant's thought that the full representational content of a perception accrues to it in virtue of distinct kinds of aspect is spot on, although there certainly are difficulties in forming an adequate and precise conception of the contribution made by sensibility.[12]

But Kant's identification of the distinctive pleasure of the beautiful depends on a rather murky conception of the mental mechanisms at work in perception of the world. For Kant identifies the distinctive pleasure of the beautiful as being the product of the two cognitive powers, the imagination, the function of which in perception is to connect and arrange the data provided by the senses to form an accurate image or perceptual representation of the object *as a piece of formed matter* as the object appears from the subject's point of view, and the understanding, the specific function of which in perception is to introduce unity into this synthesis of the sensory manifold by bringing the object under a concept of the kind of thing it is, so that the object is perceived not just as something coloured and shaped in a certain way, but as being a flower,

[11] On the conceptual or non-conceptual nature of perception and the question whether perceptual experience has a non-conceptual content see Evans (1982), Crane (1992), Peacocke (1993), and McDowell (1994).

[12] See, for example, Essay 2, III, §18.

or seashell, or whatever.[13] His claim is that the pleasure of experiencing something as being beautiful is the feeling engendered by the imagination and the understanding operating together in a particular manner, the feeling *of* this interaction, which he often characterizes in an abbreviated form as their free harmonious play. More precisely (in terms of Kant's faculty psychology): the imagination plays freely under the sole restriction that what it produces must be in harmony with the understanding's function in cognition of conceptualizing imagination's product. But even this formulation is an inaccurate representation of Kant's real view. For in the perception of a beautiful object the imagination is not truly free, since it must produce an accurate representation of the object's form on the basis of what is given in intuition: the image must be a representation of the way the object actually is, and, accordingly, the imagination is not free to manufacture whatever form it pleases but is tied to the production of a determinate form. But Kant conceives of a beautiful form as being just the kind of image that the imagination would produce if at play, under the sole constraint of conforming to the lawful nature of the faculty of understanding, i.e. under the sole restriction that its product is conceptualizable (*CJ*, 240–1).[14] So beautiful forms are just those that, under this restriction, the imagination would delight in producing if it had no other aim than to please itself. Hence, when it is required to produce such a form by a given object that confronts the perceiving subject, it freely does so in the sense that it does exactly the kind of thing that it would be disposed to do if it really were free. For this reason it is unsurprising that the subject delights in the exercise of the imagination demanded by an object with a beautiful form; and because the demands on the understanding are exceptionally slight, being required to exercise only a monitoring function, it is relatively at ease in the perception of an object as being beautiful. Putting these two factors together we reach Kant's conception of the experience of beauty as the facilitated play of imagination and understanding, mutually quickened (and so made pleasurable) by their reciprocal harmony.

[13] Kant's explanation of the pleasure that grounds a pure judgement of taste is notoriously difficult to understand, and he himself was aware of its obscurity (*CJ*, 170). His account of the nature of the pleasure taken in the beautiful is explored in Budd (2001*b*).

[14] In order to effect his deduction of judgements of free beauty it is clear that Kant requires each person's imagination to favour the production and contemplation of precisely the same perceptual forms.

This is connected with Kant's characterization of beauty as 'an object's form of *purposiveness* insofar as it is perceived in the object *without the representation of a purpose*' (*CJ*, §17, 236). Since the form of a beautiful object is one that the imagination would delight in producing if in free play, an object with a beautiful form is just as it would be if it had been skilfully designed with the express purpose of engaging the cognitive powers in free harmonious play in the contemplation of it, and in this sense the object is as though it has been designed for the express purpose of facilitating the exercise of our cognitive powers upon it. But a pure judgement of taste is not based on a concept of the object, in particular a concept of the object's purpose (or natural functions). Hence, we experience a beautiful natural object as if its form were purposive for our cognitive powers but without taking that actually to be the case (for then we would be experiencing it as art, not nature).

The fundamental difficulty with Kant's identification of the distinctive pleasure of the beautiful is that it seems to be no more than a rendition of what is undoubtedly true of the experience of finding something freely beautiful in terms of a supposed specific manner of operation of the mental mechanisms postulated in Kant's theory of perceptual knowledge—a rendition that fails to illuminate the experience. It is characteristic of the experience of finding something's form beautiful that one's attention is captured by it, so that one continues to look at the object, delighting in its appearance for its own sake—an appearance in which each part seems to answer perfectly to each other part, so that the variety in the appearance is perfectly unified, the elements manifestly according with one another or belonging together. This contemplation of the object's form requires the form's continued representation, different features of it being salient or focused on from moment to moment as one's eyes move back and forth within the object's contours as one wills. The fact that the object's delightful form continues to be represented to the subject as her eyes play over it corresponds with one feature of Kant's account, the imagination's favouring in its free play the construction of this form over non-beautiful forms, and the fact that the experiencing subject is unconcerned to identify what kind of thing the object is that possesses such a rewarding form, or unconcerned with its being the kind of thing it is recognized as being, the object in any case exhibiting a wonderfully unified array of elements, a perfect combination of unity and heterogeneity, is construed by Kant as the understanding's lacking its usual task of imposing unity by conceptualizing imagination's product. And Kant merely adds to this the idea that since the activity of each of the cognitive powers (as described) requires so little of or imposes so little constraint on the activity of the other, the activity of each is such as to quicken the activity of the other, with the result that the manner in which they jointly operate is felt as unusually delightful.[15] In so far as Kant's specification of the pleasure definitive of the experience of finding something beautiful is only a picturesque redescription of the experience, it is unenlightening; in so far as it is a matter of a priori speculation about psychological processes that occur in perception, it needs to be replaced by an empirically well-founded account.[16]

2.5. THE JUDGEMENT OF QUALITATIVE PERFECTION

Another kind of judgement—a certain kind of non-aesthetic judgement—plays a significant role in Kant's thoughts about beauty. This is a judgement about an object *as being an instance of kind K*—a judgement that, when it assumes a certain form, might mistakenly be identified with a pure judgement of taste—the judgement that the object and its parts are in harmony with, or appropriate or well suited to perform, the functions or purposes of things, or the parts of things,[17] of that kind: the judgement of *qualitative perfection*. A

[15] The idea that the understanding is quickened in the sense that it is stimulated to entertain a variety of conceptual possibilities (suggested by, for example, Allison (2001: 171)) would render Kant's account untrue to the phenomenology of the experience of the beautiful. In the experience of the beauty of an object's form, rather than entertaining various concepts under which the object might be brought, one is entirely unconcerned with how the object might be conceptualized.

[16] The effectiveness of Kant's deduction of pure judgements of taste depends on his identification of the distinctive pleasure of the beautiful being a bona fide explanation, which in turn depends on the acceptability of Kant's theory of perceptual knowledge and its postulated mental mechanisms, with objects of perception being constructed out of sensory data in accordance with the forms of space and time and a priori concepts, the imagination operating on what is given in sensibility to produce, with the aid of the understanding, experience of objects. Accordingly, a soundly based assessment of the deduction requires a deep understanding of the generation of perceptual experience by the human perceptual system.

[17] It is clear that Kant intends the concept of qualitative perfection to be applied at the level of the parts of a thing, as in the case of a flower, which is only a part of a

thing's qualitative perfection *as a K* is the suitability of its formed matter to its purpose or function as something of kind K and to the purposes or functions of its parts: to be qualitatively perfect as a K an object must be so formed that it satisfactorily discharges whatever purposes are integral to the nature of a K (*CJ*, §§15, 16, 48). (In so far as the manifold is not well suited to the object's 'purpose', or presents features antagonistic or opposed or poorly suited to it, it lacks qualitative perfection or detracts from whatever qualitative perfection the object possesses.) 'Perfect' does not mean 'could not be better'. It implies only that the object is not deformed or defective in some way that precludes a part from performing its purpose or natural function satisfactorily.

The mistaken identification Kant is concerned to oppose is that of a pure judgement of taste with a judgement of qualitative perfection when this judgement is *thought confusedly*. A concept figures in a person's judgement in a confused (indistinct) fashion if the person is not aware of and so is unable to expound the properties contained in the concept.[18] For a judgement of qualitative perfection to be thought confusedly is for the concept of qualitative perfection to figure in the judgement in a confused, rather than distinct, fashion, much as, so Kant believed, although the philosopher and the man in the street base their moral judgements concerning the wrongfulness of deceit on the same rational principles, the philosopher's are distinct, the common man's confused (*CJ*, §15, 228). For Leibniz, Wolff, and their followers, the 'sensory representation' of a characteristic *was* a confused concept of that characteristic,[19] so that, accordingly, an item's qualitative perfection as presented in perception—its looking to be, or presenting the appearance of being, well suited to discharge or perform the functions integral to the kind it exemplifies—was a confused concept of it. But a pure judgement of taste is not a cognitive judgement, not even a confused one, whereas a judgement that an object possesses qualitative perfection is a particular kind of cognitive judgement, namely a teleological judgement; and a pure judgement of taste about an object is an aesthetic judgement,

plant. In fact, Kant argues that a natural object is a natural purpose only if each of its parts has a natural function (*CJ*, §65, 373–4).

[18] See, for example, Kant (1992: 545).

[19] For Kant's critique of the view of Leibniz and Wolff that the distinction between the sensible and the intelligible is merely a matter of confused as opposed to clear representation of things see *CPR*, A43–4/B60–2.

based on the subject's pleasure in perceiving it, whereas a judgement of qualitative perfection is not an aesthetic judgement. Seeing an object as a qualitatively perfect specimen of kind K does not imply finding it beautiful,[20] and seeing it as being beautiful does not imply, for some K, seeing it as being a qualitatively perfect thing of kind K. It is therefore easy to see that the perception of an object as being beautiful is not the same as the sensory representation or 'sensuous intuition' of the qualitative perfection of the object.[21]

2.6. THE JUDGEMENT OF DEPENDENT (ADHERENT) BEAUTY

In addition to the previously mentioned non-compound kinds of aesthetic judgement, Kant acknowledges the combination of a pure judgement of taste about something with a judgement of qualitative perfection about that thing, the latter (as already indicated) being concerned with a *concept* of the kind that the object instantiates—the kind of thing it is or is meant to be. This combination of judgements constitutes another aesthetic judgement—the judgement that something is a beautiful thing of kind K—an impure judgement of taste, the judgement of 'dependent' or 'adherent' beauty.[22] Kant does not construe 'beauty' as a predicative adjective in the judgement that O is a beautiful K in the sense that he does not analyse this judgement—the judgement that O is dependently beautiful (as a K)—as the combination of the judgement that O is a K and the judgement that O is beautiful. Rather, he analyses it as the combin-

---

[20] This is easy to see from the fact that it is possible that nothing of kind K is, or is experienced by the judging subject as being, beautiful—as, perhaps, with spiders or octopuses. (Note that to judge that something is beautiful *for a K*, or *as far as Ks are concerned*, is not the same as to judge that it is a beautiful K, i.e. beautiful *as a K*.) Hegel (1975: i. 130–1) located the distinction between beautiful and ugly animal kinds (not altogether accurately) in their displaying activity and quickness of movement, 'the higher ideality of life', rather than 'drowsy inactivity', or their being of unmixed species, rather than hybrids.

[21] For Kant's justified rejection of these ideas see, for example, *FI*, §8, 'Note' and *CJ*, §15.

[22] In fact, it is not entirely clear that Kant understands a judgement of dependent beauty as a combination of these two judgements. It is possible that he requires in addition delight that the object judged is qualitatively perfect (or even delight in its qualitative perfection).

ation of the judgement that O is a good specimen of kind K and the judgement that the sensory manifold of O has a beautiful form.[23] In other words, 'O is a beautiful K' (where this expresses a judgement of dependent beauty) means 'O is a qualitatively perfect K and O is [freely] beautiful', where the first conjunct (like the second) is asserted on the basis of the look of O, so that it is apparent or manifest in O's appearance that it is a qualitatively perfect K. So a judgement of dependent beauty requires you to take into account not just the object's form but also what kind of object it is and whether it is a good specimen of this kind: an essential condition for something's being dependently beautiful is that in its appearance it should exemplify well the purpose of the kind of object it is a beautiful specimen of. Unless a thing of kind K is a good or satisfactory instance of that kind, even if it is a beautiful thing it is not beautiful *as* a K; and characteristics of an object's appearance that are not consonant with an object's function detract from the object's beauty *as* an object with that function, even if they would enhance the object's beauty if it were not considered as an object with that function.

Note that even though Kant recognizes impure aesthetic judgements about natural objects in which objects are judged under a concept, e.g. judgements of dependent beauty, this is not tantamount to countenancing the aesthetic appreciation of nature as nature (in the positive sense I have distinguished).[24] A judgement of dependent beauty made about an item of natural kind K as being an instance of that kind falls short of constituting a form of aesthetic appreciation of nature as nature: even if the kind is recognized as being a natural kind, the fact that the kind is natural is not integral to the pleasure that grounds the judgement, for only one component of a judgement of dependent beauty is itself an aesthetic judgement, and this component is just a judgement of free beauty. Accordingly, the aesthetic element of a judgement of dependent beauty is not a judgement of the object as being natural. Furthermore, to make a judgement of dependent beauty about a natural item involves,

---

[23] For Kant, beauty is always predicated of the mere form of an object, in judgements of both free and dependent beauty. The criticism that Kant's acknowledgement of judgements of dependent beauty in addition to judgements of free beauty (pure judgements of taste) introduces a contradiction into his account of beauty is easily seen to be wide of the mark. Even in a judgement of dependent beauty, the pleasure that grounds the aesthetic judgement it contains is not based on a concept.

[24] See Essay 1, §4.

for Kant, conceiving of it as a natural purpose, and so as (super-human) art. But to appreciate nature as if it were art is not to appreciate it as nature.

The notion of qualitative perfection, as it figures in a judgement of dependent beauty, suffers from a number of obscurities. The attribution of qualitative perfection in a judgement of dependent beauty will be based on the perceptual appearance of qualitative perfection. But this is susceptible of two interpretations, a weaker and a stronger, a negative and a positive. The weaker requires only that the appearance should not be such as to indicate an imperfection in the proper functioning of the parts. In other words, it does not look as if some part of the object is not well suited to perform its natural function. The stronger demands more: the object must display signs that its visible parts are well suited to discharging their natural functions. But now consider the body of an animal, for example. Which parts with natural functions can visibly be performing (or appearing to perform) their function well? The skin, the nose, the ears, the eyes, the lips, the arms? It is easy to see that a bodily part is deformed or missing, but the lack of such defects does not constitute qualitative perfection. Does the sheen of a young person's hair or the bloom of his or her complexion, each an indicator of health, signal that the hair and skin are performing their own specific natural functions well? Moreover, the natural function of a bodily part, the arm, for example, can be manifold, and the part can be well suited to perform some, but not all, its functions. Furthermore, the stationary or momentary appearance of an animal's body is not in general a good guide to whether certain of its visible parts are in good condition—to whether the eyes can see or the hands can grip—this being manifest only in movement. In what follows I shall ignore all such difficulties (except the last).

Note that the combination of judgements that constitutes a judgement of dependent beauty does not, as such, involve a twofold pleasure. For the perception of an object as being qualitatively perfect need not occasion pleasure. A qualitatively perfect specimen of natural kind K is one in which each part is performing satisfactorily or outstandingly well its natural function or 'purpose'. To see a natural object as a qualitatively good or perfect specimen of its kind is to see the various manifest parts of the object as being well suited to perform their natural functions. But seeing a natural item as being a qualitatively perfect instance of its kind implies neither of the two forms of delight that might be occasioned by its qualitative perfection: pleasure that the item is a qualitatively perfect specimen of kind K or pleasure in the item's qualitative perfection as a K. To take pleasure in its qualitative perfection as a K, in its being a good specimen of its kind, is to take pleasure in the perception of its various parts as being well suited to perform their natural functions, to delight in its manifold as being good for a K (*CJ*, §16, 230–1); and such a pleasure is not an inevitable consequence of the perception of its qualitative perfection. And the perception that something is a qualitatively perfect thing of its kind need not occasion pleasure that it is such a specimen. Nevertheless, although the combination of judgements that form a judgement of dependent beauty does not, as such, involve a twofold pleasure, it allows for such a possibility. The possibility that Kant recognizes (*CJ*, §16) is that delight in an object's beauty might be conjoined with delight that the object is a qualitatively perfect K.[25] But for Kant pleasure that something is qualitatively perfect is an intellectual, rather than an aesthetic, pleasure: a pleasure is aesthetic only in virtue of being the determining ground of a judgement, and pleasure that an object is a qualitatively perfect thing of its kind is not the determining ground of the judgement that it is such a qualitatively perfect specimen. Accordingly, this twofold pleasure is a combination of pleasures of different kinds, neither of which, Kant maintains, is enhanced by being combined with the other, although the union of the two pleasures constitutes a heightening of the subject's total experiential state (*CJ*, §16).

2.7. UNACKNOWLEDGED AESTHETIC JUDGEMENTS ABOUT NATURAL THINGS

Although Kant regards every living thing, a thing that is both organized and self-organizing, as being a natural purpose, in which every

[25] Note that, for Kant, pleasure that something is a qualitatively perfect K can never be universally valid, for he often stresses that there is no necessary connection between the applicability of a concept and the feeling of pleasure—no rightful demand that everyone should experience pleasure—except in the case of the morally good, and he characterizes pleasure that an object is qualitatively perfect as pleasure based on a concept. This would also apply to pleasure in an object's qualitative perfection.

part of the thing is a purpose, he does not maintain that it is mandatory that judgements about their beauty should be constrained by
their 'intrinsic purposiveness', so that all such judgements must be
judgements of dependent beauty. On the contrary, it is allowable to
ignore their being natural purposes and consider just their form. In
fact, Kant claims that aesthetic judgements about the beauty of
natural objects are typically pure judgements of taste (judgements of
free beauty).[26] Accordingly, he insists (rightly) that judgements about
the beauty of flowers characteristically do not involve a judgement
about the suitability of the flower to its discharging its natural function (as the reproductive organ of the plant), a function that a great
many who experience flowers as beautiful might well be ignorant of,
and which a botanist pays no attention to when judging the beauty of
flowers (*CJ*, §16) (although it is certainly possible to delight in a
beautiful flower's suitability to performing its sexual function, as
when its structure is wonderfully well suited to the distribution of
its reproductive cells by a particular insect). Kant recognizes, however, that our aesthetic judgements about the beauty of natural
objects are not always pure judgements of taste: he acknowledges
that our aesthetic judgements about the beauty of certain kinds of
natural objects, above all sentient things (horses or human beings, for
example), are usually judgements of dependent or adherent beauty
(*CJ*, §§16, 48). But in cases where an aesthetic judgment about a
natural item's beauty is not a judgement of free beauty, Kant's
account does not in fact seem to be an accurate analysis of the
judgement's content, for it is not a constituent of the judgement
that someone is a beautiful man or woman that his or her form—
considered independently of its being the form of a man or the form of
a woman—is beautiful.[27] This defect stems from Kant's conception

---

[26] It has often been argued that Kant is mistaken about this. But in fact it is not
important whether Kant is right about the normal application of the concept of
beauty to natural items. The crucial issue is not whether our normal aesthetic judgements about flowers, for example, are in conformity with Kant's view, or, indeed,
whether we ever judge flowers as free beauties. For even if we rarely or never judge
natural objects, or natural objects of a certain kind, as free beauties, this would show
only that Kant was mistaken about the frequency of pure judgements of taste about
natural objects. What matters is not whether our aesthetic judgements about natural
objects are typically pure judgements of taste, but whether Kant's classification of
aesthetic judgements about natural objects accurately identifies all significant forms of
the aesthetic appreciation of nature. In what follows I indicate my scepticism.

[27] In one place (*CJ*, §48, 312) Kant claims that the content of 'That is a beautiful
woman' is just 'Nature displays in that woman's form a beautiful presentation of the

of a judgement of dependent beauty as a conjunction of two judge-ments, one being aesthetic—a pure judgement of taste—and the other non-aesthetic, which is forced upon him by his leading idea that beauty is properly predicated only of an object's form. Accordingly, in a judgement of dependent beauty about an object of natural kind K beauty is related to the natural kind only externally, not internally: Kant cannot acknowledge the idea of an object's being beautiful *as* a K. Although this is a consequence of Kant's conception of beauty as properly predicated only of an item's form, considered in abstraction from the kind of thing it is, it reveals a gap in Kant's classification of aesthetic judgements, perhaps a twofold gap, even if his doctrine about the proper subject of beauty is accepted.[28]

For what this classification fails to recognize is the possibility of a certain kind, or more than one kind, of non-compound aesthetic judgement about a natural object *as being an instance of kind K*.[29] First, there is a kind of aesthetic judgement about a living thing as being an instance of its natural kind, a judgement that concerns its qualitative perfection. Now for there to be a distinctive judgement for which the subject's pleasure is a determining ground—the judge-ment that something is funny, for example—the thought-content of the judgement must be resistant to specification independently of the nature of the subject's hedonic reaction. Unlike the judgement that something is pleasant or the judgement that something is beautiful, the thought-content of the judgement that something is qualitatively perfect can be specified independently of the nature of the subject's response to the object and so of any reference to pleasure. Hence it is not an aesthetic judgement. But a judgement that asserts the cap-acity or suitability of a natural item's qualitative perfection to give pleasure has the required response-dependent thought-content.

---

purposes inherent in the female figure'. In short: to judge a woman to be a beautiful woman is to judge her figure to be a beautiful presentation of the purposes inherent in the female body. And this means that her figure is such as to satisfy the natural functions of the female body and it is beautiful. Note that Kant here omits any reference to the expression of morally desirable qualities as a requirement of female beauty (see §8).

[28] It is clear that the idea of a judgement of dependent beauty needs to be relativ-ized to moments in time, most obviously so if the judgement is about a living thing capable of locomotion. For there is no such thing as the form of such an organic being: its bodily shape and the relations among its bodily parts change not merely in virtue of its ageing but as it moves. And the different shapes it might assume—as when a bird folds or unfurls its wings—will not in general be equally beautiful.

[29] This possibility is explored in Essay 1.

A judgement of this kind satisfies Kant's criterion for a judgement to be aesthetic, but is missing from Kant's classification. Of course, not all qualitatively perfect objects are likely to be judged as suitable to give pleasure in virtue of their qualitative perfection, no matter what natural kind they belong to. Rather, a judgement of this sort—one that expresses delight in an object's qualitative perfection as a K— will depend on the character of the natural functions of a certain natural kind and the ways in which they are realized in the appearance of something of that kind. Furthermore, if the natural function of a part or parts of the body of an animal or insect is to enable the creature to move around its environment, as with the wings of a bird or butterfly, the fitness of the parts to perform their natural function will be manifest only when the creature is in motion through the use of those parts. In such a case, delight in the qualitative perfection of a creature with respect to these parts will be taken not so much or at all in the creature's stationary appearance (or its appearance in motion through the use of other parts of its body) but in the display of the parts' fitness to discharge their natural function; and the delight will be dependent on the creature's manner of movement, as with the gracefulness of a gazelle's leaping motion or the speed and power of a galloping horse, or the manifest suitability of the bodily parts to the creature's ability to flourish in its natural environment, as with the wings of an eagle or a hummingbird. Second, not every kind of natural thing is, as such, a thing with natural functions: natural items divide into those that do possess natural functions—living things, things of a kind that have evolved by natural selection—and those that do not. Clouds, mountains, rainbows, volcanoes, sunrises, stalactites, and many other natural items do not have natural functions and are not composed of parts that perform such functions. And yet aesthetic delight in them can be delight in them *as things of such kinds.* Kant's aesthetic theory fails to countenance the possibility that aesthetic pleasure might be derived from the formed matter of an object seen as falling under a non-purposive, non-functional, concept, so that its being something of that kind is integral to the pleasure.[30] But there is nothing in his

---

[30] Of course Kant recognized that there are natural objects which are not purposive (in form) (see, for example, *FI*, §6); but he does not seem to have contemplated the possibility that any such objects might be aesthetically attractive as being instances of their kinds—that their aesthetic appeal might be dependent upon their being seen as certain kinds of thing.

conception of an aesthetic judgement as a judgement whose determining ground cannot be other than the feeling of pleasure or
displeasure that implies that an aesthetic judgement must be based
on a consideration of an object in abstraction from what kind of
thing it is or any concepts under which it falls.[31]

2.8. AN IDEAL OF BEAUTY

A further judgement of beauty that Kant identifies is the judgement
that an item of kind K is an *ideally beautiful K*. It might be thought
that, since the judgement that O is dependently beautiful as a K
includes the judgement that O is qualitatively perfect as a K, the
judgement that O is dependently beautiful as a K is the same as, or at
least implies, the judgement that O is an ideally beautiful K. But this
is not so: an object can be a dependently, but not an ideally, beautiful K. In fact, even if there are innumerably many dependently
beautiful Ks, no one of them might be an ideally beautiful K, the
idea lacking any application. For there is an ideal of beauty for
things of kind K if and only if it is possible for there to be a
maximally beautiful thing of that kind, a unique, exemplary archetype of beauty—something that is such that, unless a thing of kind K
matches it in appearance, that thing is a less [dependently] beautiful
thing of kind K.[32] In other words, there must be a specific form that

---

[31] Paul Guyer (1996: 103) has suggested that it follows from Kant's definition of an
aesthetic judgement as a judgement the determining ground of which cannot be other
than subjective, which therefore cannot be a concept, that the determining ground of
an aesthetic judgement must be pleasure in the mere representation of an object. But
the fact that a concept cannot be the determining ground of an aesthetic judgement
does not imply that the determining ground must be pleasure in the mere representation of an object. For pleasure taken in the representation of an object under a
concept is subjective, not objective, and the determining ground of a judgement
based on such a pleasure would be the pleasure, not the concept.

[32] In fact, Kant does not spell out exactly what he means by an ideal of beauty for
things of kind K. That he means a maximally beautiful K is indicated by his asserting
that 'the highest model, the archetype of taste', the ideal of the beautiful, 'does indeed
rest on reason's indeterminate idea of a maximum' (*CJ*, §17, 232). I ignore the
possibility that Kant's conception of an ideal of beauty is less demanding, allowing
that there is an ideal of beauty for things of kind K if there are maximally beautiful
Ks—things of kind K than which nothing of kind K can be a more beautiful K—of
quite different forms. This appears to be ruled out by various details of Kant's
thoughts about an ideal of beauty; and if this were his conception, these thoughts
would be even less compelling than, I believe, they are.

something of kind K can possess, which is such that anything of kind K that possesses that form is more beautiful than anything of kind K that does not. This requires that the natural functions or 'purposes' of things of that kind must so constrain the appearance of those things whose parts perform these functions well as to determine a particular form that such a thing must assume, if it is not to fall short of the beauty attainable by things of that kind.[33]

Kant denies that there are any natural kinds other than humanity that are subject to such a severe constraint, so that there is just one kind of thing that admits of an ideal of beauty, namely a human being. Clearly, as Kant asserts, there cannot be an ideally beautiful tree, a tree with a form more beautiful than any other possible form that a tree might have: the requirement of presenting the appearance of satisfying the natural functions of the elements of a tree allows too much latitude in form for trees to admit of an ideal of beauty. And the same is true for other natural kinds that have many different varieties. But the more specific the species, the less numerous the possible variations in form among equally beautiful instances of the species; and the concept of an ideally beautiful thing of a certain kind appears not to contain anything that would in principle rule out an ideal of beauty for a highly specific type of organism, each part of which has a natural function.

Furthermore, Kant's claim that there is an ideal of human beauty is unconvincing in a number of ways. There is some uncertainty in his conception of an ideally beautiful human being, but he appears to represent the ideal of human beauty as being the product of two factors, the 'aesthetic normal idea' of the animal species *Homo sapiens* and the visible expression in the human body of the qualities of a person who has a morally good soul. The normal idea of the adult human body,[34] which a human body must not violate if it is to

---

[33] This formulation is an accurate representation of Kant's thought only if the notion of *purpose* is not restricted to natural functions of bodily parts but has the wide scope given to it by Kant, for whom it includes the idea of humanity's moral 'vocation'. In fact, Kant considers human beings to be an exception to the rule that no natural kind admits of an ideal of beauty just because human beings are persons, moral agents: this is their sole relevant distinguishing feature. His introduction of the appearance of moral goodness into the ideal human figure is, of course, motivated by the requirement of qualitative perfection, not by beauty of form.

[34] Kant omits the requirement that the normal idea of the human body as it figures in the ideal of human beauty should be the normal idea of the qualitatively perfect human body. But unless this condition is imposed, his idea that 'conformity' with the

be beautiful,[35] is a kind of stereotype of the appearance of a human being, formed in the imagination, Kant speculates, in a manner similar to the way in which the image in a Galtonian composite photograph is created. But he himself acknowledges that different races and cultures will form different normal ideas of the adult human species, a particular body that conforms to one such idea violating another, and he ignores the obvious fact that humanity comprises both men and women, whose bodies possess parts with different natural functions (although it is clear that this should be written into Kant's account).[36] And even if there were to be a unique normal idea of the human species, this would not secure the desired consequence that there is a maximally beautiful form of a human being, even leaving aside what Kant considers to be the all-important contribution of morality to the ideal beauty of a human body. For the inevitable indeterminateness of the normal idea of a natural kind—a feature that Kant's position requires—will accommodate different but equally beautiful forms of instances of that kind, thereby violating the requirement of uniqueness of form for ideal beauty. Moreover, there are many features of the human body that the requirement of qualitative perfection does not determine: size or shape of head, length of neck, relative proportions of lower to upper leg, of trunk to legs, and so on. Hence, indefinitely many qualitatively perfect human bodies will diverge from the form given by the normal idea, and Kant fails to establish that any such human body must be less beautiful than a human body of the form realized by the normal idea. Furthermore, unless there is only a single way in which the qualities of a morally good soul can be manifest in

normal idea of the human body is a necessary condition of human beauty is unpersuasive. Kant maintains that to be a beautiful K is to be a qualitatively perfect K and to have a beautiful form. Hence, conformity with the normal idea of a K is a necessary condition of being a beautiful K if and only if every qualitatively perfect K must conform with the normal idea of a K. But this will not be so unless the normal idea of a K is understood as the normal idea of a qualitatively perfect K—if even then.

[35] The normal idea of the human body does not constitute the complete ideal of human beauty but 'only gives the form that constitutes the indispensable condition of all beauty'. Moreover, Kant maintains, the reason we are pleased by the normal idea is only because 'it does not contradict any of the conditions under which alone a thing of this kind can be beautiful', not because it is itself beautiful (*CJ*, §17, 235). Accordingly, Kant conceives of the normal idea as a template that an object must 'fit' if it is to be a beautiful instance of its kind.

[36] I ignore the fact that the form of the human body varies as its limbs and other movable parts are differently disposed, an important feature for Kant given the fundamental role of form in his account of beauty.

any form (above all, that of the human face) that is consonant with the normal idea, the essential contribution of morality to the ideal of human beauty will further undermine the required uniqueness of the type of an ideally beautiful human being.

2.9. INTERESTED AND DISINTERESTED PLEASURES

Kant maintains that the pleasure expressed in a pure judgement of taste is disinterested. He explains an interest in an object as pleasure in the [representation of the] object's existence (*CJ*, §2, 204, §4, 209, §41, 296).[37] What he means by this is that an interested pleasure in an object is pleasure *that* such and such is the case with respect to the object: it is pleasure that the world is a certain way, pleasure that something is true of this particular object, pleasure in a *fact* (or apparent fact) about the object; in particular, pleasure that a certain kind of thing, which the given object exemplifies, exists. Pleasure at the existence of O is pleasure that such-and-such is (positively) the case with respect to O, which is pleasure at a fact (or apparent fact) about O. Kant passes freely between the conception of an interest as a propositional pleasure and the conception of an interest as a desire or concern that something should be the case, a desire determined by a concept (e.g. *CJ* §4, 209, §10, 220). This move is easy to understand, for if you are pleased that p you want it to be the case that p, and if you want it to be the case that p and you believe that p then you are pleased that p. His claim about a pure judgement of taste is therefore that the pleasure it expresses is not pleasure that the represented object exists, or that it is of a certain kind or possesses certain properties, which implies that the pleasure is not the satisfaction of one of the subject's desires. Given Kant's understanding of a pure judgement of taste as a judgement about an item's form based on the pleasure experienced in the contemplation of that form, this is clearly correct: pleasure *in* the perception of an object's structure is not the same as pleasure *that* the elements of the object are structured as they are.

---

[37] In fact, as a number of commentators have pointed out, Kant explains the notion of an interest in a number of different, and apparently non-equivalent, ways, or appears to operate with more than one sense of the notion; and to many his meaning has not appeared obvious.

It is unclear whether Kant conceives of pleasure in an object's qualitative perfection as being an interested pleasure.[38] But given his concept of an interest, it would be wrong to construe this pleasure as an interest: pleasure in O's qualitative perfection is not identical with pleasure in the fact that O is qualitatively perfect (which pleasure could arise for a variety of reasons), and implies neither this nor any other merely propositional pleasure. However, it is clear that Kant must allow for the combination of pleasure in the beautiful and an interested pleasure—as he does when delight in an object's beauty is conjoined with pleasure that it is a qualitatively perfect thing of its kind. Consider another case: you are delighted at or in seeing your first instance of something of a certain kind, which you also find beautiful to behold. Your pleasure has a double source and a double object: it derives both from your awareness of the fact that you are seeing for the first time an object of kind K and from the inherent beauty of the specimen before you; and you are delighted by both the fact and the beauty of the item. In fact, leaving aside pleasure in the agreeable and pleasure in the morally good, Kant should allow for a threefold combination of pleasures, two being disinterested and one an interest: pleasure in an object's qualitative perfection, pleasure in its beauty, and pleasure in the existence of the object—as, for example, when you are delighted by the manifest suitability of a bird's make-up to the performance of the various natural functions of its parts, by the beauty of its form, and by the fact that your longstanding desire to see a bird of that kind (a hen harrier, for instance) has at last been realized. Additional pleasures are also possible, e.g. higher-order pleasures (pleasure in the communicability of one's pleasure, for example). But there is no need to argue that Kant must allow for the combination of an interested pleasure and pleasure in the beautiful, for Kant construes the lover of natural beauty— someone who has an immediate interest in natural beauty—as deriving pleasure not only from a natural object's beauty but from the object's existence. And Kant's thoughts about the conditions of an immediate interest in natural beauty and its importance in human life form the final part of his account of the aesthetic appreciation of nature, as far as beauty is concerned.

---

[38] Kant certainly claims that pleasure based on the concept of a purpose is interested: 'Whenever a purpose is regarded as the basis of a pleasure, it always imports an interest as the determining ground of the judgement about the object of the pleasure' (*CJ*, §11).

II.   Kant on Natural Beauty and Morality

> her supple Brest thrills out
> Sharpe Aires, and staggers in a warbling doubt
> Of dallying sweetnesse, hovers o'er her skill,
> And folds in wav'd notes with a trembling bill,
> The plyant Series of her slippery song.
> Then starts shee suddenly into a Throng
> Of short thicke sobs, whose thundring volleys float,
> And roll themselves over her lubricke throat
> In panting murmurs, still'd out of her Breast
> That ever-bubbling spring...
>
> Richard Crashaw, 'Musicks Duell'

2.10.   A PURE JUDGEMENT OF TASTE DOES NOT, OF ITSELF, GENERATE AN INTEREST

Kant maintains not only that the pleasure expressed in a pure judgement of taste is not an interest, i.e. the determining ground of the judgement is a *disinterested* pleasure, but that such a judgement is not inherently *interesting*, i.e. in or of itself it does not generate an interest (*CJ*, §2 n., 205). This thought underlies his remarkable tripartite claim about natural beauty to the effect that someone who takes an immediate interest in natural beauty can do so only in virtue of possessing at least the germ of a morally good disposition; someone who is in essence a morally good person cannot reflect on natural beauty without this reflection generating an immediate interest in natural beauty; and it is right to demand that each person take such an interest. For at the bottom of Kant's thoughts about the possibility, inevitability, and significance of an immediate interest in natural beauty is the idea that an explanation is needed of a person's interest in natural beauty—an explanation other than the fact that the experience of beauty is pleasant. This idea is implied by Kant's bald assertion that a pure judgement of taste does not, of itself, give rise to any interest; and by this he means that the pleasure that is the basis of a judgement of taste does not itself give rise to an interest. Clearly, it is Kant's identification of pleasure in the beautiful as pleasure in free beauty that leads him to claim that pleasure in the beautiful of itself does not generate an interest. For pleasure in free beauty is pleasure that is independent of any concepts under which the object is experienced, but an interest is pleasure in the instantiation of a concept, pleasure that the concept is instantiated in the object of one's judgement.[1]

Given the ease with which Kant shuttles back and forth between the conception of an interest as a propositional pleasure and the conception of an interest as a desire (under or determined by a concept), and that Kant sometimes means more by someone's taking an interest in natural beauty than the person's being pleased that it exists—he means also that the person desires to experience it and so willingly gives time to seeking it out—it is important to distinguish three desires that might be associated with the pleasure of experiencing something as beautiful. These are (i) a desire to continue to look at the beautiful object, (ii) a desire to look at other objects with the same form, and (iii) a desire to look at other objects of the same non-formal kind. Kant's conception of pleasure as self-sustaining[2] requires him to acknowledge that pleasure in a beautiful object encourages a desire of the first kind, the desire to keep looking at the object, and he does acknowledge this: '[pleasure in the beautiful] does have a causality inherent in it, namely that of *preserving* the state of the representation itself and keeping the cognitive powers engaged without any further aim. We *linger* in our contemplation of the beautiful, because this contemplation strengthens and reproduces itself' (*CJ*, §12). But it is clear that there is no inherent connection between the pleasure of experiencing something as

---

[1] Pleasure in a beautiful form is not pleasure that such a form is instantiated. As I have already indicated (Essay 2, I, §9), when the lover of natural beauty comes across a beautiful natural item, her pleasure is both interested and disinterested. It is interested in that she delights in the existence of the object, and it is disinterested in that she derives pleasure from the form, independently of her desire to find such an object or that there should be such an object, or in addition to her pleasure that this beautiful item exists where she is. It follows that, for Kant, pleasures must be individuated at least partly by reference to what it is that a pleasure is pleasure in (its intentional object).

[2] For example: 'Consciousness of a representation's causality concerning the subject's state as tending to *preserve the continuation* of that state, may here be said to designate generally what is called pleasure' (*CJ*, §10, 220).

being beautiful and desires of the second or third kind: the experience of finding the form of an object beautiful need not engender a
desire to experience other objects with that form; and pleasure in a
beautiful object of a certain kind does not in itself provide a reason
to desire to experience other objects of the same non-formal kind—a
desire for anything of that kind—in the expectation that it will be
equally beautiful, for the pleasure is pleasure in the object's form and
other objects of the same non-formal kind might not have that (or
another) beautiful form.

In fact, there seems to be no relevant difference between pleasure
in the beautiful and pleasure in the agreeable with respect to the
second kind of desire: the experience of finding the matter of
an object pleasant need not engender a desire to experience other
objects with that matter. And just as the experience of finding the
form of an object beautiful might, but might not, generate the desire
to experience other objects with different beautiful forms, so the
pleasant experience of one kind of matter might, but might not,
generate the desire to experience pleasurable matter of different
kinds. However, Kant maintains that a judgement of the agreeable
differs from a judgement of the beautiful in that it, unlike a judgement of the beautiful, 'expresses' an interest in its object, giving as
his reason that by means of sensation such a judgement arouses a
desire for objects of that kind:

Now, that a judgement by which I declare an object to be agreeable
expresses an interest in it is already obvious from the fact that, by means
of sensation, the judgement arouses a desire for objects of that kind, so that
the delight presupposes something other than my mere judgement about the
object: it presupposes that I have referred the existence of the object to my
state insofar as that state is affected by such an object. (*CJ*, §3)

What is Kant's point here? Consider pleasure in the sweetness of a
taste. It would be a mistake to identify pleasure in the sweetness
of a taste with pleasure in the taste's being an instance of that kind
(i.e. being sweet), which pleasure is pleasure in the taste as falling
under that concept: this would be to confuse pleasure in its sweetness
with pleasure in its being sweet. And it would be a mistake to
conflate (i) pleasure in its being an instance of that kind (= an
interested pleasure), and (ii) its arousing a desire for something
(more) of that kind, or to infer (i) from (ii). Hence, even if Kant
were right that a judgement that something is agreeable arouses a

desire for other objects of that kind, pleasure in the agreeable is not an interested pleasure, given Kant's conception of an interest. But in any case it is not an invariable truth that pleasure in an object as being agreeable arouses a desire to experience immediately, soon after, or ever, other objects of the same agreeable kind: inhaling the odour of a flower with delight does not necessarily set up a desire to repeat the experience.

But the vital point concerning beauty is that the possession of the capacity to make pure judgements of taste and familiarity with its exercise does not imply as a matter of necessity the existence of an interest in experiencing freely beautiful objects. For, apart from any other considerations, in general the capacity to experience pleasure of a certain kind does not necessarily go hand in hand with an interest in experiencing such pleasures—on the contrary, one might want not to experience any pleasures of that kind; and pleasure in the beautiful is no exception to this general truth, being compatible with a negative interest in its object; that is, displeasure at its existence. In this sense Kant is clearly right to claim that a pure judgement of taste does not, of itself, generate an interest.

2.11. AN IMMEDIATE INTEREST IN NATURAL BEAUTY

It is vital for Kant that a person's immediate interest in what she takes to be beautiful nature should be dependent on its being nature, so that if she were to be taken in by a cunning artificial replica her interest would disappear if she were to learn the truth:

if we were to play a trick on our lover of the beautiful, by planting in the ground artificial flowers (which can be made to look very like natural ones), or by perching artfully carved birds on the branches of trees, and he were to find out how he had been taken in, the immediate interest that he previously took in these things would vanish at once . . . A bird's song proclaims joyousness and contentment with its existence. At least we interpret nature in this way, whether or not this is its purpose. But it is the indispensable condition of the interest which we here take in beauty [that is, the beauty of a bird's song] that the beauty should be that of nature; it vanishes completely as soon as we realize that we have been deceived, and that it is only a product of art—so completely that even taste can then no longer find anything beautiful in it nor sight anything attractive. What do poets praise more highly than the night-ingale's bewitching and beautiful song in a lonely thicket on a still summer evening by the soft light of the moon? And yet we have instances of a jovial landlord, where no such songster was to be found, playing a trick on the guests staying with him to enjoy the country air—to their great satisfaction—by hiding in a bush a roguish youth who (with a reed or rush in his mouth) knew how to reproduce this song in a manner close to nature. But as soon as one realizes that it is all a fraud, no one will long endure listening to this song which before was regarded as so attractive. And it is just the same with the song of any other bird. It must be nature, or be taken by us for nature, if we are to be able to take an immediate *interest* in the beautiful as such; and this is all the more so if we can require others to take a similar interest too. And such a demand we do in fact make, for we regard as coarse and ignoble the habits of thought of those who have no *feeling* for beautiful nature (for this is what we call the susceptibility to an interest in the contemplation of beautiful nature), and who confine themselves to the mere enjoyments of sense found in eating and drinking. (*CJ*, §42, 299, 302–3)

Here we find a number of claims or suggestions that need to be disentangled. First, there is the idea that we experience the sounds of a bird's song *as beautiful* only if we hear them as being naturally produced.[3] But this suggestion conflicts with Kant's inclination to regard our judgements of natural beauty as being, typically, judge-ments of free beauty (in the strong sense that the judgement is not based on the object's being seen as falling under any particular concept of the object). Furthermore, the *form* of a bird's song does not seem to change if heard, first as naturally produced, second as artificially produced. Accordingly, given Kant's understanding of beauty as properly predicated only of form, he cannot without contradiction hold that the sounds are heard as beautiful only if heard as being naturally produced. Independently of this specific point, it should be clear that even the delight in natural beauty of Kant's lover of natural beauty, who has an immediate interest in natural beauty, does not for Kant constitute aesthetic appreciation of nature as nature (in the positive sense). For it consists of two components, one aesthetic, the other not: a disinterested pleasure in an object's form and an interest in the object's being natural. Hence, it is not integral to the aesthetic delight that the object is natural, or is of a certain natural kind.

[3] The generalization of this claim—that a natural item is experienced as beautiful only if it is experienced as being natural—is clearly untenable.

Then there is the suggestion that the appeal of birdsong is due to its being heard *as if it were emotional expression*.[4] Although this seems here to be offered as an adjunct to its beauty, perhaps it is intended as an alternative explanation of its appeal. This interpretation receives some confirmation from an earlier passage about birdsong:

> Even a bird's song, which we can bring under no musical rule, seems to have more freedom, and thus to be richer for taste, than the human voice singing in accordance with all the rules of the art of music; for we grow tired much sooner of frequent and lengthy repetitions of a human song. Yet here we probably confuse our participation in the joyfulness of a dear little creature with the beauty of its song, for if exactly imitated by man (as has sometimes been done with the notes of a nightingale) it would strike our ear as completely lacking in taste. (*CJ*, 'General Remark on the First Section of the Analytic', 243)

Here Kant appears to claim either (this is the obvious reading) that a bird's song (the song of a nightingale, for example) is not beautiful—the impression that it is arising only because we confuse our empathic (or sympathetic) response to the bird's (supposed) joy with our finding the song beautiful—or that it is heard as beautiful only if heard as produced by a bird. The first alternative would imply that someone who takes an immediate interest in a bird's song—an immediate interest in it only because it is natural—is not thereby someone who has an immediate interest in natural *beauty*. And this suggestion seems right. For rarely, if ever, does a bird's song have, in comparison with indefinitely many products of the art of music, any marked degree of beauty; and our delight in a bird's song is either delight in a series of sounds with at least some small degree of beauty being a product of nature, not art, or a function not at all of whatever beauty it might have, but of our interpretation of it as expressing the bird's vitality.

But these are minor matters necessitating, at most, only the omission of birdsong and other non-beautiful but emotionally expressive natural phenomena from the catalogue of beautiful natural phenomena in which an immediate interest might be taken. What

---

[4] The clear recognition of this might well have led Kant to acknowledge kinds of aesthetic judgement about natural items that are missing from his classification (see the considerations in Essay 2, 1, §7). Not all poets have thought of attractive birdsong as expressing a bird's joy in life: 'The bird knows nothing of gladness | It is only a song-machine' (George McDonald).

is fundamental is the requirement that the immediate interest taken in beautiful natural objects must be based solely on the thought that the beauty is nature's handiwork. Kant's crucial claim is that it is a necessary condition of our taking *an immediate interest* in the beautiful as such that we should take it to be nature, *a fortiori* if we are to be justified in demanding of others that they also should take such an interest; and, Kant maintains, we do make such a demand on others, as is shown by the fact that we regard the habits of thought of those who (i) do not take an immediate interest in beautiful nature, and (ii) devote themselves instead to 'the mere enjoyments of sense found in eating and drinking', as 'coarse and ignoble'.

Kant thinks of an immediate interest in beautiful nature as being connected only indirectly with someone's finding something beautiful. The interest is immediate in that it is an interest in beautiful nature in itself, not for any further reason,[5] and in particular not because it is thought of as being connected with the morally good; the connection is indirect in the sense that it is not generated by a pure judgement of taste as such (even one that is made about an object that is known to be natural), but is mediated by natural beauty's suitability to be linked to the morally good. And the connection between natural beauty and morality is a priori, not empirical:[6] an interest in natural beauty is aroused in virtue of an a priori connection between the experience of finding a natural object beautiful and the feeling of pleasure in being aware that our action is in conformity with what morality requires of us (positive moral feeling).

[5] Kant understands the idea of an interest in something *in itself* in such a way that an interest in something intentionally designed to delight (as being so intentionally designed) is not an immediate interest (*CJ*, §42). It is this that enables him to deny the possibility of an immediate interest in beautiful art. (Note that someone might be pleased that a beautiful natural object exists in a certain place without this interest being *immediate*, as when it is in the financial interest of a curator of a public park who is not a lover of natural beauty that there should be a beautiful natural object in a certain position in the park.)

[6] Kant identifies an empirical interest in the beautiful that we possess in virtue of being members of society (*CJ*, §41). Our sociability—our propensity and suitability for society—entails a concern not just to give pleasure to others, but especially for those pleasures in which each person can share, pleasures that are universally communicable. But pleasure in the beautiful is just such a pleasure. Hence, our sociability leads us to beautify ourselves and our surroundings, to present ourselves to others in an aesthetically attractive manner by dressing in beautiful clothes and adorning ourselves and our homes with beautiful objects. But this empirical interest is not at the heart of Kant's philosophical concerns; it is focused on art rather than natural beauty; and Kant's attitude towards it is in fact equivocal.

2.12. MORALITY AND AN IMMEDIATE INTEREST IN NATURAL BEAUTY

Why is an immediate interest in natural beauty—a desire[7] to find and experience natural beauty, for no reason other than admiration and love of natural beauty, and even at some cost to oneself—an indication of moral worth? How exactly do the two factors, an item's naturalness and its beauty, explain the connection between the desire and moral worth? The intentional object of desire (or pleasure) is an item of natural beauty—which, for Kant, regarding it as free beauty, means that it is such as to provide a disinterested pleasure in its perceptual form, which is experienced as exhibiting purposiveness but is not regarded as in fact having any purpose or having been produced by a will, this disinterested pleasure not *as such* producing an interest. What is definitive of the virtuous person is her motivation. For Kant, the motivation of the morally good person is duty for duty's sake—which he interprets as meaning that the agent acts in virtue of her judgement as to the 'form' of her maxim, namely that it is such that it can be willed as universal law, the judgement not being founded on an interest *but producing one*. Kant's position appears to be that a person who reflects on the beauty of nature will take an immediate interest in natural beauty if, and only if, she has at least the germ of a good moral disposition.[8] In itself the second part of this position is insubstantial, since nearly all adult human beings possess the germ of a good moral disposition, and perhaps most in a somewhat developed form. This part of Kant's

[7] As I indicated in Essay 2, 1, §9, Kant slips freely between the idea of interest as desire, and the idea of interest as pleasure in the existence of. So, on the second reading, he asserts that one who takes an immediate interest in natural beauty is not only 'pleased with nature's product for its form, but is also pleased at its existence . . . without connecting that existence with any purpose whatsoever' (*CJ*, §42, 299).

[8] The necessary condition: 'someone who takes such an [immediate] interest in the beautiful in nature can do so only insofar as he has previously solidly established an interest in the morally good. Hence if someone has an immediate interest in the beauty of nature, we have reason to presume that he has at least the basis of a good moral disposition' (*CJ*, §42, 300–1). The sufficient condition: 'the mind cannot reflect on the beauty of *nature* without at the same time finding its interest aroused' (*CJ*, §42, 300). Kant claims that if an immediate interest in natural beauty is *habitual* and readily associates itself with the contemplation of nature, this indicates at least a temper of mind favourable to moral feeling (*CJ*, §42, 298–9); and that someone with fine artistic judgement who willingly abandons beautiful art for beautiful nature has a beautiful soul (*CJ*, §42, 300).

position gets its bite from the claim that it is the possession of this potentiality—this and only this—that can explain anyone's taking an immediate interest in natural beauty. In support of his view he appears to present a main and a supporting argument, the first claiming to establish one part of his position, the second responding to a predicted scepticism about a crucial element in the first argument.

The first runs something like this (*CJ*, 300–1): As moral agents we necessarily have an interest in the 'objective reality' of our moral ideas, which means that we have an interest in nature's showing some trace or giving a hint that it is in harmony with the ends of morality. So we must take an interest in any manifestation in nature of a harmony that resembles that harmony. But the existence of natural beauty is such a manifestation. Hence, we cannot reflect on the beauty of nature without at the same time finding that we take an interest in it. But this interest is akin to moral interest (pleasure in the existence of morally good actions). And someone who takes an immediate interest in natural beauty can do so only in so far as he or she already has a solidly based interest in the morally good.

This argument begins by deriving an interest in natural beauty from our desire to find nature in harmony with our moral ends, by way of a kinship or inner affinity between the two interests, and then proceeds to the conclusion that an interest in natural beauty is possible only for someone with a solidly based interest in the morally good. A peculiar feature of the argument is that it just slips in the claim that a *necessary* condition of someone's taking an immediate interest in natural beauty is their already having a solidly based interest in morality on the coat-tails of the conclusion that it is a *sufficient* condition of someone who has an interest in morality taking an interest in natural beauty that they should reflect on natural beauty. And the argument for this conclusion is itself questionable. The idea is that a moral agent must have an interest in nature's showing some trace or giving a hint that it is hospitable to the ends of morality, and so must take an interest in any manifestation in nature of a harmony that resembles that harmony. But, as far as Kant's argument goes, the existence of natural beauty, which renders nature not alien to humanity and can foster our sense of belonging to it, reveals only that nature is hospitable to the aesthetic exercise of our cognitive powers. The affinity it indicates between humanity and the natural world concerns not our ability to realize our moral ends, but the satisfaction of our desire for beauty.[9] And Kant offers no reason why nature's (ample) satisfaction of our desire for beauty should be taken as indicative of its being in harmony with the ends of morality. The resemblance of two harmonies is not the same as identity and does not guarantee that an interest in one of them will engender an interest in the other. Furthermore, supposing it were possible that nature should not contain beautiful natural forms, the attainability of the ends of morality would, it would seem, be just the same, just as easy or difficult, as in the real world. So the existence of natural beauty should not be taken as an intimation of nature's being sympathetic to the attainment of those ends. The fact is that (external) nature can be neither hostile nor hospitable to anything required of us by morality.

Kant takes the affinity between pleasure in the form of a natural object and moral feeling that he has identified as being 'the true interpretation of that cipher through which nature speaks to us figuratively in its beautiful forms' (*CJ*, 301). In defence of this interpretation he returns to the analogy between a pure judgement of taste and a moral judgement: a pure judgement of taste is a judgement about not the matter but the form of an object, namely its suitability to give universal pleasure; a moral judgement about the rightness or wrongness of acting from a certain principle is a judgement about not the matter but the form of the principle, namely its suitability to be willed as a universal law;[10] and neither judgement is based on what the subject desires. The point of analogy that Kant highlights and wishes to exploit[11] is the fact that, despite

[9] In the *Critique of Teleological Judgement* Kant argues that organisms must be thought of as possible only as natural purposes; that this entails that we should think of all of nature as a system of purposes of nature; and that this allows us to regard nature as having favoured humanity by displaying so many beautiful shapes, which is something for which we may love nature (*CJ*, §67). But, apart from any other consideration, the premise is not now plausible.

[10] In fact, there is an ambiguity in the notion of form. The form of a beautiful object is *the structure of its elements* (in virtue of which it is suited to please each person); but the form of a maxim or principle of action just is *its accordance or conflict with the requirement of willed universality*, its suitability or unsuitability to be willed as a principle that each person acts from.

[11] Given the tensions apparent in Kant's text, similarities between certain of his thoughts about the lover of natural beauty and thoughts he later offers in explication of the claim that beauty (whether of art or nature) is the symbol of morality (the morally good), and the fact that beauty (whether of art or nature) is always construed by Kant as beauty of form, it might be thought that there would be nothing amiss in reading some points of analogy between beauty and the morally good indicated by

their differences, both kinds of judgement represent a pleasure—in the one case, pleasure in an object's form, in the other, pleasure in a morally good action—as being universally appropriate, the right response to the object of the judgement (the first of these pleasures being disinterested, the second an interest). His claim is that this analogy leads a certain kind of person, one who thinks in a morally good way or would easily be trained to do so, to take just as strong an immediate interest in natural beauty as in morally good actions, this effect being produced without the person needing to engage in any distinct, subtle, and deliberate process of reflection. This appears to mean that a lover of natural beauty does not need to have identified any of the points of analogy Kant indicates in order for the analogy to have generated his or her immediate interest in natural beauty. And Kant certainly regards the ordinary person's concepts both of beauty and the morally good as being 'confused' or 'indistinct',[12] thus precluding an articulated awareness of these points of analogy. But it is unclear exactly how Kant conceives of the analogy's bringing about the effect he attributes to it. Must the lover of natural beauty be aware in some sense that there is an analogy, even if the thought is 'confused'? Does the analogy need to operate at a conscious level at all? Perhaps his view is that anyone who experiences disinterested pleasure in the perception and con-templation of beautiful natural objects and who is inclined to the morally good will inevitably be led to take an interest in natural beauty through the person's unarticulated awareness of a parallel between, on the one hand, moral *feeling* ('the susceptibility to feel pleasure or displeasure merely from being aware that our actions are consistent with or contrary to the law of duty' (Kant 1991: 201)), i.e. the susceptibility to an interest in morally good actions, and, on the other hand, a *feeling* for natural beauty, i.e. the 'susceptibility to an [immediate] interest in the contemplation of beautiful nature'

Kant in support of the idea that beauty is the symbol of morality back into the earlier discussion of the lover of natural beauty. For Kant, the crucial feature of beauty in virtue of which it is a symbol of the morally good is the *freedom* integral to the recognition of beauty: on the one hand, there is the free play of the imagination (within the bounds imposed by the lawful nature of the understanding) that is consti-tutive of the experience of beauty; on the other, the freedom of the will (in which the will is a law to itself) that is required by the morally good. But importing this parallel into the consideration of the lover of natural beauty would not seem substantially to strengthen Kant's arguments.

[12] For an explicit recognition of this character of the concept of beauty as possessed by someone who cannot expound its elements see Kant (1992: 545).

(*CJ*, §42, 303), without this parallel being the person's reason for taking such an interest. But Kant is silent about this.

However, even if the analogy Kant indicates is somehow conducive to the effect he desires, this does not establish that a person who takes an immediate interest in natural beauty must be someone who has a commitment to morality or at least a high potential for developing such a commitment, for there might be alternative ways in which an interest in natural beauty can be generated. Neither does it show that such a morally sensitive person who meditates or reflects on natural beauty must or is even likely to develop an interest in natural beauty: at most, it shows how such a person might develop this interest, although a real understanding of the growth of such an interest out of a process of meditation or reflection on natural beauty stands in need of a characterization of the content of this process. And the additional consideration that Kant brings forward—that our failure to find the purpose underlying the purposiveness of beautiful natural forms outside us (in nature's purpose) naturally leads us to look for it in ourselves, in the ultimate purpose of our existence, our moral vocation, the requirement to be a morally good person, to possess a good will (*CJ*, 301)—manifestly fails to strengthen his position. For, apart from any other consideration, this assumes that we are compelled to locate a purpose of natural beauty somewhere—a purpose that concerns human beings—an assumption that is unfounded. Hence, Kant's attempt to establish that moral feeling is a necessary and sufficient condition for a feeling for natural beauty is not compelling.

The third element in Kant's tripartite claim about the love of natural beauty is that we are right to demand that each person take an immediate interest in natural beauty. In other words, each person ought to take such an interest.[13] But to be justified in demanding that each person take an immediate interest in natural beauty it would not be enough (nor would it be necessary) to establish that only habits of thought trained to the morally good or highly susceptible of such training can explain the existence of an immediate interest in the beauty of nature, and will produce such an interest in a morally decent person who reflects on natural beauty. Rather, what is required is a convincing argument to the conclusion that an immediate interest in natural beauty, however this might

---

[13] Although Kant does not explicitly make this claim, it is clear that he acquiesces in our making this demand (*CJ*, §40, 296, §42, 302–3).

come about, *encourages* the development of moral feeling in an especially effective manner. For it is only if an immediate interest in natural beauty makes one into or encourages or makes it easier for one to become a morally good person that a good case can be made for the cultivation of an appreciation of natural beauty, and even so this will not be an overwhelmingly strong case unless what a love of natural beauty achieves can be gained in no other way, or not so easily. It is clear that Kant desires this conclusion, especially because it would allow the pure judgement of taste to effect a transition from perception of and delight in the natural world to moral feeling. He asserts (*CJ*, 'Introduction', IX, 197) that the harmonious operation of sensibility and understanding in the experience of beauty promotes the mind's receptivity to moral feeling, making the concept of a purposiveness of nature a suitable mediating link between the realms of nature and freedom. He claims that the disposition 'to love something (e.g. beautiful crystal formations, the indescribable beauty of plants) even apart from any intention to use it' 'greatly promotes morality or at least prepares the way for it' (Kant 1991: 237). And he asserts that 'The beautiful prepares us to love something, even nature, apart from any interest' (*CJ*, 'General Remark on the Exposition of Aesthetic Reflective Judgements', 267). But there is a crucial difference between loving something *apart from* any interest and being happy to act *contrary to* strong self-centred desires or other desires that conflict with the requirements of morality. For a love of natural beauty to be well suited to foster the development of morality it would, on Kant's conception of morality, need to make one receptive to the call of reasons for action that are not based on one's desires. But delight in natural beauty has nothing to do with reasons for action. Since Kant was fully aware of this it is no wonder that his assertion is soon followed by:

It is true that the immediate pleasure in the beautiful in nature presupposes and cultivates a certain *liberality* in our way of thinking, i.e. makes our delight independent of any mere enjoyment of sense; but here freedom is still represented more as in *play* than as exercising a law-ordained *function*, which is the genuine characteristic of human morality, where reason must exert its dominance over sensibility. (*CJ*, 268–9)

Whether the preparation for morality that Kant has in mind concerns the preparation of children for entry into the moral world or the preparation of those within the moral world to give precedence

change, they remain a unity. An ideal human being is one in whom each member of these pairs, freedom and necessity, change and unity, is combined with the other member—the will freely obeys the law of necessity and reason maintains its rule through every change in experience, desire, and feeling. By 'the law of necessity' Schiller means the fundamental principle of morality, which, in virtue of our possession of freedom of the will, it is always possible for each of us to act in accordance with, and which is such that it is necessary that we should do so. And we will not be divided selves, in which feeling and reason pursue their separate goals, if we always do what morality requires us to do, not because we are pulled one way by our feelings or desires but another by our reason, but because our desires and feelings are shaped by and so do not run counter to morality. Schiller's idea is that the self-division from which we suffer, as beings who are both sensuous and moral, is to be replaced not by a return to a state of naive nature, one that we were in as children, unselfconscious, at one with ourselves, no self-reflection intervening between instinct and action precisely because we lacked the capacity to reflect on ourselves, but by progress to a reunified sensibility, a state of equilibrium of our sensuous and rational aspects, a complex unification of the two sides of our nature, in which there is no conflict between feeling and thought, our feelings having been moulded to harmonize with morality and our thoughts expressing themselves in appropriate action through these feelings. In the terms of *On the Aesthetic Education of Man* (Schiller 1982), the ideal of human life is to be a person in whom the two fundamental human drives, the sensuous and the rational, are both fully developed and in perfect harmony, the capacity to think and act rationally exercising an uncoerced authority over a rich, flourishing, animal vitality nourished by experience, morality no longer being a constraint on desire and feeling, which have been so educated as to be instinctively in accordance with the requirements of duty.

Like Kant, Schiller insists that the particular feeling of delight in nature that he has in mind would be destroyed if what was taken to be a natural thing were discovered to be an artificial replica of it. But, although Schiller credits Kant with being the first person to reflect on the significance of the distinction between a natural item and a perfect imitation of it, Schiller's concern with love of nature is very different from Kant's: whereas Kant's is the love of natural *beauty*, Schiller's is the love of *naive nature*, which might well have little beauty, and in any case is not loved for being a beautiful product of nature. And their conceptions of an interest in nature—for Kant, natural beauty, for Schiller, naive nature—are significantly different: whereas Kant regards pleasure in the existence of natural beauty as not being itself a moral satisfaction, Schiller maintains that pleasure in naive nature is a moral satisfaction.

But how convincing is Schiller's account and explanation of the love of nature merely because it is nature? The natural things that he takes to have a claim on our love include sentient things, non-sentient living things, and lifeless things. He maintains that what we love in naive nature is something we now lack. His description of this character includes 'the silent creative life' and 'their acting serenely on their own', which, taken more or less strictly, would appear to apply only to living things, and must be understood as signifying projections on to nature of desirable human characteristics. It is therefore unsurprising that the two characterizations he highlights—'inner necessity' and 'eternal unity with themselves'—are the ones that seem to have an all-embracing scope. But what exactly do they mean?

'Inner necessity' and 'eternal unity', as Schiller understands them, are not entirely different things but different aspects of a single thing. We, unlike anything non-human, are free in that we are free to act in accordance with whatever principles we choose, and from time to time we change the principles that we act from. So we lack the necessity of acting in accordance with any particular principle and the unity of always acting from the same principle. The sense in which the ideal human being does not change is that there is no change in the principles that determine his or her behaviour, which is mirrored in the natural world by non-human sentient creatures being determined by their instincts and needs, by non-sentient organic things having a principle of growth built into them as things of a particular natural kind, and by inanimate things being determined by their intrinsic physical nature and the unchanging laws of physics.

But if this is what Schiller has in mind,[15] his conception of the love of naive nature appears extravagant. First, do we ever see a rock or a

[15] Frederick Beiser (1998: 228) interprets Schiller's conception of (naive) nature as representing 'a state of complete independence, of total self-sufficiency, the absence of need and constraint', which is manifestly false of animal life, and identifies the state we lived in as children as one of 'complete independence because we were in harmony with ourselves, with others, and with the external world', a state that no child lives in.

stream as representing Schiller's conception of naive nature and love them for this idea that they represent? There has never been a moment in my life when I have done so.[16] Second, abstracting, as we must do, from any aesthetic appeal they might have, do non-sentient animate things, flowers or trees, for example, or sentient things, such as birds and bees, when we are delighted by their being natural, evoke our love for their 'inner necessity' and 'eternal unity with themselves'—characteristics shared with inanimate things? Is it not rather for what is distinctive of them—for their being forms of life? Some of us have a respect for life in all, or at least many, of its forms and can experience delight in its manifestation, no matter how meagre its aesthetic attractiveness, merely because it is a living thing—not merely because it is natural. But perhaps this is to miss Schiller's intention. For in what must be regarded as a special case, young children, his observations, which are acute, acknowledge the distinctive character of the objects that evoke the feeling for nature that he is concerned with. The case of children is especially instructive, for in addition to the contrast between their naturalness and our artificiality Schiller also indicates their as yet unlimited potential as contrasted with our now limited condition, which always falls short of what was possible. When, at certain moments, we are overcome with tenderness in the presence of children, Schiller rightly asserts that the feeling is not adequately thought of as resulting only, or even at all, from the idea of a child's helplessness. Rather, it is the idea of the child's 'unlimited determinability' and innocence that touches us, as is clear from our emotion's being delight mixed with a certain melancholy. Whereas a child's potential is 'infinite', ours is limited by what we have become and inevitably falls far short of the human ideal; and whereas our experience is such as to make us inwardly divided, a young child, lacking the capacity to reflect on itself, suffers from no divided consciousness. Nevertheless, to generalize from children to other animate things, sentient and non-sentient, and also to inanimate things, building into our response the distinctive character of the object, will not, I believe, render plausible

[16] It is unclear exactly what Schiller has in mind by the love of nature, merely as such. Hardly anyone, perhaps nobody, experiences love for a piece of matter, an undistinguished bit of rock, say, merely because it is natural. If what he had in mind had been being in nature, free to walk or stop where one pleases, without coming across humanity or any signs of it, there would be more plausible explanations of the satisfaction than its being moral—freedom from the requirements of morality, for example (leaving aside possible moral demands of non-human sentient nature).

Schiller's conception of our feeling for nature (merely because it is nature) being a mixture of the melancholy and the sublime in virtue of these natural items representing an idea of what we once were and what we should strive to become.[17]

---

[17] Schopenhauer's explanation of our delight in observing animals (Schopenhauer 1974: ii. 582–3) hits the nail on the head. Our pleasure in watching the 'highest and cleverest animals' is pleasure in the 'complete naïveté of all their expressions', i.e. their inability to dissimulate; and the pleasure in watching every free animal, a bird, frog, hedgehog, weasel, roe, or stag, pursuing its life is due mainly to the fact that we are 'delighted to see before us our own true nature [the will-to-live] so greatly *simplified*'.

III. Kant on the Sublime in Nature

Ma sedendo e mirando, interminati
Spazi di là quella, e sovrumani
Silenzi, e profondissima quiete
Io nel pensier mi fingo; ove per poco
Il cor non si spaura.

Giacomo Leopardi, 'L'infinito'[1]

in all time,
Calm or convuls'd—in breeze, or gale, or storm,
Icing the pole, or in the torrid clime
Dark-heaving;—boundless, endless, and sublime—
The image of Eternity...

Lord Byron, *Childe Harold's Pilgrimage*

2.13. INTRODUCTION

In her classic study of the development of the feeling of the sublime
in external nature (Nicolson 1959), Marjorie Hope Nicolson argues
convincingly that the main difference between English seventeenth-
and eighteenth-century attitudes towards and experiences of landscape and former attitudes was not due to the rediscovery of the
rhetorical theories of Longinus. Rather:

Awe, compounded of mingled terror and exultation, once reserved for God,
passed over in the seventeenth century first to an expanded cosmos, then
from the macrocosm to the greatest objects in the geocosm—mountains,
ocean, desert. (143)

In other words, an emotion thought appropriate to God was transferred to the immensity of interstellar space and then to the vastest

---

[1] 'But as I sit and gaze, in my mind I imagine endless spaces beyond, and super-
human silences, and profoundest quiet; wherefore my heart almost loses itself in
fear.'

known terrestrial objects. Accordingly, such objects, especially mountains, were experienced as symbols of eternity and infinity, and in contemplating them the mind ascended from mountains through the immensity of space to eternity and infinity, 'with awe and reverence for the power of God, to the serene and tranquil peace that passes all understanding' (393).

Kant's theory of the sublime in nature takes on board some of the features assigned to it by his predecessors, reinterprets others, and introduces new ideas: it is a kind of secularized and moralized version of 'The Aesthetics of the Infinite'. Although it disassociates the sublime from God, it retains a link with morality and, in an unprecedented manner, actually strengthens the connection with the notion of infinity. Rather than merely thinking of the experience of the sublime as a derivative of the experience of God, it requires the experience of the sublime to involve the idea of infinity: the sublime is defined in terms of infinity. It takes over the dual nature attributed to the emotion of the sublime in seventeenth- and eighteenth-century English thought—one with both a positive and a negative aspect—but offers a new interpretation of the nature and genesis of each of its aspects. Furthermore, it distinguishes two forms of the sublime, each concerned with the immensity of nature merely as that immensity appears in perception independently of how the nature that possesses that immensity is conceptualized; it identifies the imagination as the source of the experience of the sublime in both forms; and it offers an account of the imagination's working as it strives to come to terms with the sheer immensity presented by nature.

I propose not to take issue with two features of Kant's account of the sublime in nature: first, its linking of the sublime to the idea of immensity, and, second, its representation of the emotion of the sublime as consisting of two aspects. Rather than questioning whether something other than immensity can properly trigger the experience of the sublime, and rather than questioning whether the emotion of the sublime must involve both a positive and a negative side, I prefer to restrict attention to the aesthetic experience of immensity and, within the set of possible emotional responses to immensity, to focus on a distinctive double-aspect response involving both pleasure and pain. I also propose to leave unquestioned the independence of Kant's two forms of the sublime, the mathematically sublime, which is concerned with the immensity of nature in its extent, and the dynamically sublime, which is concerned

with the immense power of nature.[2] Even within these limits I believe
that Kant's theory contains a number of mistaken elements, in
particular the binding of sublimity to infinity, the account of the
operation of the imagination in the experience of the sublime, and
the characterization or characterizations of the double-aspect emotion of the sublime.

2.14. KANT'S CLASSIFICATION OF PURE AESTHETIC JUDGEMENTS OF THE SUBLIME

For Kant, a pure aesthetic judgement of the sublime is a singular,
categorical judgement, that is not based on an interest in or a
concept of the object it is occasioned by, and that proclaims itself
universally valid. In these respects it resembles a pure judgement of
taste. But Kant's fundamental thought about the sublime in nature
is that, unlike beauty, sublimity cannot properly be predicated of
any natural object. One of his reasons for holding this is that
'sublime' is a term of approval, but in itself an object that precipi-
tates the feeling of the sublime is experienced as 'contra-purposive'
for ourselves as embodied subjects, appearing incommensurate with
our sensory or physical powers, and as it were violating our imagination (at least in one form of the sublime). Properly speaking, such
an object can be said only to be suitable for inducing in us a feeling
of sublimity, a vivid consciousness of a respect in which we are
sublime, a feeling of our own sublimity as rational agents. A related
difference between the beautiful and the sublime is that whereas
natural beauty maintains the mind in restful contemplation, the
sublime in nature stimulates a 'movement' of or 'agitation' in the
mind. Hence, since the feeling of our own sublimity is pleasurable,
the movement of the mind provoked by the sublime in nature must
in some way be 'subjectively purposive', either with respect to our
power of cognition or with respect to our faculty of desire—it must
induce pleasure in virtue of its consequences with respect to the
sensuous and intellectual elements of perceptual knowledge (on
the one hand, sensibility or the imagination, on the other, thought

---

[2] For a contrary view see Bradley (1909), where Bradley assigns priority to the idea
of power, mere magnitude of extension evoking the sublime only in virtue of being
('insensibly') construed as a sign of immense power.

or the understanding) or with respect to our capacity for rational action. The first yields the mathematically sublime, the second the dynamically sublime.[3] Each form of the sublime involves (i) an estimation (or awareness) of nature's immensity, (ii) an operation of the imagination, (iii) a felt inadequacy in our power with respect to nature, and (iv) a compensating superiority over nature. But they differ in the character of what is estimated, the activity of the imagination, the inadequacy, and the superiority. The mathematically sublime is concerned with the estimation of nature's size, the dynamically sublime with an awareness of nature's might; in the mathematically sublime the imagination figures in an 'aesthetic' estimation of magnitude, in the dynamically sublime in an appreciation of force; whereas the inadequacy experienced in the mathematically sublime is an inability of the imagination, it is one of physical resistance in the dynamically sublime; and, finally, the mathematically sublime evokes a sense of the superiority of one of our mental faculties (thought) over another (sensibility), but the dynamically sublime makes palpable to us our status as moral agents, a status of incomparable value that is denied to nature. In each case, the vivid awareness of a manifest inability to cope with nature, which is experienced with pain, is the occasion of a vivid awareness of an aspect of ourselves that is superior to any aspect of nature, and this is experienced with pleasure (albeit—at least for the dynamically sublime—a 'negative pleasure', admiration and respect).

2.15. THE MATHEMATICALLY SUBLIME

Kant defines the mathematically sublime as what is absolutely great or large, great beyond all comparison, i.e. in comparison with which everything else is small. It follows at once that nothing in nature that

[3] It is clear that Kant often forces his material into a framework that more naturally fits his account of the mathematically than the dynamically sublime—as his opening elucidation of the sublime in terms of unboundedness to which the thought of its totality is added (*CJ*, 244), which is incorporated into the analysis of the judgement of or pleasure in the sublime with respect to the so-called 'quantity' of such judgements, indicates—although his determination to link the experience of the sublime to morality is, as I later claim, allowed to distort his account of the mathematically sublime. In what follows in the text I attempt to steer a course that by and large ignores these deformations, and this necessitates my turning a blind eye to certain nuances of Kant's thought.

can be 'given' in perception, nothing that can be an object of the senses, is properly characterized as [mathematically] sublime.

Kant's account of the mathematically sublime is based on a distinction between two ways of estimating or judging an object's size—an aesthetic or a [mere] mathematical estimation of magnitude. Now to judge how large anything is, we need something else in terms of which we measure it, and this unit of measure will itself have a magnitude. The distinction between the two forms of judging size is that an aesthetic, but not a mathematical, estimation of magnitude must be made by the eye, without the aid of measuring instruments, on the basis of the object's appearance in mere intuition, which requires that the unit of measure is itself 'aesthetic', something that can be comprehended in one intuition. Kant claims that all estimation of the magnitude of natural objects is ultimately aesthetic, and that whereas no greatest unit of measure is possible for the mathematical estimation of magnitude, there is a greatest for the aesthetic estimation of magnitude, namely the most that can be grasped in a single intuition. The truth behind the first claim is a minor matter and easy to see, but the nature and status of the second, which plays a crucial role in Kant's account, is more elusive.

To estimate the size of an object is to judge how many times bigger or smaller it is than a certain unit of measurement. But unless you know how big this unit is, knowing an object's size in terms of this unit does not enable you to know how big the object is—whether it is bigger or smaller than a mountain or a molehill. And the additional knowledge required is not a matter of knowing the unit of measurement's size relative to some other unit of measurement. Rather, you must grasp how big some unit of measurement is in the sense of being able to apply that unit to the size of objects on the basis of perception, i.e. to demonstrate how big the unit is by indicating some object in your environment as being the same size as the unit or some fraction or multiple of it. Such an ability is fundamental in understanding how big or small something is on the basis of its measurements. This is the truth underlying Kant's claim that all estimation of the magnitude of natural objects is ultimately aesthetic.

Although he is not explicit about this, by an aesthetic estimation of magnitude Kant means an estimate, by the eye, of how many times greater (or smaller) the perceived object is than some aesthetically grasped unit of measure. Kant's claim that there is a greatest aesthetic unit of measure is based on his conception of an extensive magnitude. For Kant, a magnitude is extensive if the representation of the parts makes possible, and therefore necessarily precedes, the representation of the whole. Spatial objects are extensive magnitudes, and so can be intuited only through successive synthesis of part to part (*CPR*, A162–3/B203–4). To take in a quantum by intuition, so as to be able to use it as a unit of measure for the estimation of magnitude, the imagination must engage in (i) apprehension (of the manifold of intuition) and (ii) comprehension: it must successively represent the parts of the given manifold and it must put them together in a single intuition. Apprehension can be carried on *ad infinitum*, but comprehension soon reaches its maximum, the most that can be grasped, retained, held together, in one intuition, yielding an impression of the whole, a visual impression of the entire expanse that was apprehended, a visual impression that encompasses the whole expanse. It reaches this maximum because a point is reached at which any advance in apprehension can be secured only at the expense of a loss in comprehension of what was earlier apprehended as this disappears from the imagination (*CJ*, 251–2): beyond this point one no longer has an impression of the whole and so lacks a sense of the distance from one end of the manifold to the other. And this maximum is the aesthetically greatest measure for the estimation of magnitude.

It might seem natural to understand this conception of the greatest aesthetic unit of measure as the idea of some (finite) size beyond which the imagination (a particular person's imagination or any person's imagination) cannot comprehend the size of something in one intuition—some maximally comprehensible size. But this would be a mistake.

Consider, first of all, how Kant believes that the existence of a maximum aesthetic unit of measure explains Savary's observation in his *Letters on Egypt* that to gain the full emotional effect of the Pyramids, it is necessary to look at them neither from too near nor from too far (*CJ*, §26, 252). The reason Kant advances is that if they are viewed from too far away, the parts to be apprehended, the tiers of stone, are only obscurely represented, and their representation produces no effect on one's aesthetic judgement; but if they are viewed from too near, the time needed by the eye to complete the apprehension from base to apex is too great for the comprehension ever to be complete, i.e. for the size to be comprehended in a single intuition. Kant does not explain himself further, and I am sceptical of his claim to explain Savary's observation. But two things are clear. First, Kant is assuming that the unit of measure is the height of a tier of stones. The obscure representation of the tiers of stone consists in its being unclear either where the divisions are (and so how many tiers there are) or how big they are. But if the unit of measure is the height of a tier of stones, we can't see how many units compose the height of a Pyramid if we can't see where the divisions are; and if we can't see where the divisions are, we can't see how great this unit of measure is. Accordingly, from too great a distance we can't use the height of a tier of stones as an aesthetic measure of the height of a Pyramid. Second, to estimate the size of an object aesthetically it must be possible to comprehend it in a single intuition, which for a Pyramid is possible from a distance, but not possible from a position so close that it necessitates the Pyramid's being scanned from bottom to top in too great a time: to estimate the magnitude of an object aesthetically is to be able to *see* that it is so many such-and-such units of measure. In other words, as Kant understands the idea, in an aesthetic estimation of magnitude the object whose magnitude is to be estimated must itself be comprehended through the synthesis of a number of its parts equal in size to the unit of measure (for otherwise estimation by counting through progressive apprehension would always be possible, no matter how big the object might be).

This brings out a point that Kant neglects to emphasize in his account of the mathematically sublime, but which is of vital importance, namely that how much of the visual field an object occupies—and so how much of it can be taken in in a single intuition—varies with its distance from the viewer: the more distant it is, the less it occupies; and no matter how large an object may be, it can be accommodated within one's visual field if it is far enough away (and emits or transmits enough light). This implies that to have a sense of the size of a very distant, massive object that, because of its immense distance, occupies a relatively small portion of the visual field, it is necessary to imagine how big it would look if seen from closer to. It also implies, first, that an aesthetic estimate of an object's size is bound up with an estimate of its distance, and, second, that, given the satisfaction of the condition concerning light, the magnitude of any object, however immense, is in principle available as an aesthetic unit of measure. But how far away something is cannot always be seen: its perception is dependent on various factors other than its distance, and these are not always present. And if you cannot see how far away an object is (the moon or a star, for example), you cannot see how big it is or estimate its size relative to other objects whose distance also cannot be seen. This radically affects the adequacy of the idea of an aesthetic estimation of magnitude as it is used by Kant in his account of the mathematically sublime.

So Kant's idea of there being a maximum for the unit of measure for an aesthetic estimation of magnitude is not the idea of there being, for each human being, some size beyond which such a unit cannot be comprehended by the imagination in a single intuition. Rather, it is the idea that, if, in the circumstances, a proposed unit of measure takes too long to apprehend, it cannot on that occasion be used as a unit of measure in an aesthetic estimation of magnitude. Associated with this is the idea that for any given aesthetic unit of measure there is a maximum size that the imagination can comprehend *using this unit as measure*; correlatively, for any given magnitude to be estimated aesthetically, the unit of measure in terms of which it can be estimated cannot be too small. Accordingly, as the magnitude to be estimated aesthetically increases, so must the unit of measure. It follows that if the magnitude is infinitely great, an attempt to estimate that magnitude aesthetically must end in frustration. If, therefore, we are prompted by nature to encompass an aesthetic unit of measure appropriate to the infinite, we will be engaged on an impossible task that will sooner or later expose the limitation of the imagination, and so our power of aesthetically estimating the magnitude of things in the world. It is precisely this that induces the experience of the mathematically sublime—or so Kant maintains.

This interpretation is, at least in part, borne out by a revealing, although somewhat uncertain, passage:

Examples of the mathematically sublime of nature in mere intuition are all those cases in which the imagination is given, not so much a larger numerical concept, as a large unit as measure (to shorten the numerical series). A tree judged by the height of a man gives, at all events, a standard for a mountain; and if the mountain is a mile high, it can serve as a unit for the number that expresses the earth's diameter, so as to make it intuitable. The earth's diameter can serve similarly for the known planetary system; this again for the Milky Way system; and the immense number of such Milky Way systems, called nebulae, which presumably form a system of the same kind among themselves, does not lead us to expect any boundaries here. Now in the aesthetic estimation of such an immense whole, the sublime lies not so much in the greatness of the number, as in the fact that the farther we advance, the larger are the units we reach. (*CJ*, 256)

Kant here indicates that the larger the object the magnitude of which is to be estimated aesthetically, the larger must the unit of measure be. And, remarkably, in this passage he seems to be happy with the idea of aesthetically estimating the magnitude of a mountain by that of a tree, the diameter of the earth by the height of a mountain, the extent of the solar system by the earth's diameter, the size of our galaxy by that of the solar system, and so on.[4] But, more significantly, having begun by identifying instances of the mathematically sublime in nature as cases in which the imagination must use a large unit as measure in the aesthetic estimation of magnitude, it turns out that it is the limitlessness, or the apparent limitlessness, of the universe that, so it seems, is responsible for the experience of the sublime. For it is only in the aesthetic estimation of *its* magnitude, not in the aesthetic estimation of the size of a tree, a mountain, the diameter of the earth, the solar system, the Milky Way galaxy, or any other system which has limits, that there is no end to the increasing size of the unit of measure that the imagination must encompass. Why and how is the infinite—Kant runs together the ideas of the infinite and the unlimited—implicated in the generation of the experience of the sublime when I am confronted by an immense object, but not by the limitless whole of the universe?

It is hard to make plausible sense of Kant's theory. The fundamental line of thought runs along these lines: An aesthetic estimate of magnitude involves the choice of a certain unit of measure and an estimate by sight of the magnitude of the given object as a certain multiple of this unit. But we can do this (fairly easily) only for small multiples: the unit of measure for the aesthetic estimation of an object's magnitude must not be too small relative to that magnitude. So the larger the object, the larger the unit of measure required to estimate its magnitude by sight. In other words, the aesthetic estimation of the magnitude of larger and larger objects requires the comprehension of progressively larger units of measure. But in the

---

[4] At *CJ* 254, however, Kant asserts that although the earth's diameter can be apprehended, it cannot be comprehended in a single intuition. Presumably he is thinking of travelling the distance of the earth's diameter: in doing so one would apprehend its magnitude, but not comprehend it.

experience of the mathematically sublime we are driven to try to make the unit of measure ever greater, beyond the imagination's capacity. We are driven to attempt this by reason, which demands totality for all *given* magnitudes: for, according to the doctrine of the first *Critique*, if the conditioned (of whatever kind) is given, a regress in the series of its conditions is set us as a task.[5] This demand applies even for those magnitudes that can never be completely apprehended, although in sensory representations they are judged as completely given. And this demand requires comprehension in one intuition, embracing all the members of a progressively increasing numerical series, not exempting the infinite (space and past time),[6] which we must regard as completely given. But the infinite is absolutely great—Kant's opening definition of the [mathematically] sublime[7]—and it cannot be thought as a whole by using a standard of sense, an aesthetic unit of measure, for this would require the comprehension in one intuition of a magnitude that is a definite proportion of the infinite, an incoherent notion. Hence, nature is sublime in those of its phenomena that in their intuition convey the idea of their infinity, which is so only when the greatest effort of the imagination is unable to estimate the magnitude of the object aesthetically, when the aesthetic estimation of magnitude cannot but be defeated.

This line of thought (of which I have omitted certain curious details) is multiply problematic, even within the terms of Kant's own philosophy. One idea contained in it is that the infinity of space is completely 'given', which recalls the assertion in the 'Transcendental Aesthetic' of the first *Critique* that 'Space is represented

[5] For the application of this principle to space see *CPR*, A412–13/B439–40.

[6] Although Kant's definition of the mathematically sublime as what is absolutely great applies as well to past time as to space, and although the magnitude of past time is just as suitable a cause of the experience of the sublime as the magnitude of space, it would not be easy to apply or adapt Kant's account of the mathematically sublime, with its emphasis on the insufficiency of a sensory standard for the aesthetic estimation of magnitude, which is designed to capture the experience of the sublime with respect to space, to cover the experience of the sublime evoked by a vivid awareness of the immensity of past time. A problem in extending any account of the sublime to past time arises from the fact that if the appreciation of the sublimity of past time is properly to be thought of as aesthetic it should, it seems, be based not on the mere thought of the immensity of past time, but on the experience of the passage of time.

[7] If the mathematically sublime is the infinitely great, only the universe as a whole (that is, the entirety of space, as thought of by Kant) qualifies—and that is something that cannot be seen, and its magnitude, therefore, is not susceptible of aesthetic estimation.

as an infinite *given* magnitude', 'for all the parts of space coexist *ad infinitum*' (*CPR*, A25/B40). Kant does not elaborate this thought, but for it to be relevant to the mathematically sublime it must refer not to the infinite divisibility of space, but, as I take it to do, to its infinite extent. It is Kant's view in the first *Critique* that although space (the geometry of which is Euclidean) is infinite, the world, the magnitude of which is not given to us in an intuition, cannot be said to be finite or infinite in extent (*CPR*, A523–5/B551–3; A519–20/ B547–8). Leaving this aside, however, and granting Kant that in our understanding of nature we are subject to the demand for a regress *in infinitum*, or, if not *in infinitum*, at least *in indefinitum* (*CPR*, A512– 13/B540–1), there is no good reason why this demand should be applied to the aesthetic estimation of magnitude, which idea is essential to Kant's understanding of the mathematically sublime. Even if, as the first *Critique* maintains, in the understanding of nature I am compelled to seek ever further for the conditions of the given conditioned, and so for 'absolute totality' and the uncon- ditioned ('conceived as containing a ground of the synthesis of the conditioned') (*CPR*, A321–4/B377–80, A409/B436), this is a require- ment only on how I must *think* about nature. Accordingly, I cannot think of space as having limits or the world as having limits in space. But the question that Kant gives no satisfactory answer to is this: Given that I am concerned to form an aesthetic estimate of the magnitude of an object that confronts me, why should its immense size impose upon me the requirement to attempt to estimate aesthet- ically not its own magnitude, but an infinite magnitude, a task that requires an impossible aesthetic unit of measure and so violates the imagination? Furthermore, there is no object that can be given in intuition that conveys the idea of *its own* infinity (rather than the limitlessness of space), and no object, no matter how large it may be, can *seem to be* unlimited; and Kant appears to hold (although this may be an aberration) not that there are natural objects whose magnitude cannot be estimated aesthetically, but that the magnitude of any particular object can be estimated aesthetically, given that it transmits enough light to the eye to be seen and can be compared in size with an object of lesser magnitude. It might well be that some- times the magnitude of an object prompts an observer to think of the limitlessness of space. But when this does happen, it would be highly unusual for an observer—even one with the level of cultural devel- opment Kant takes to be necessary to be disposed to experience the feeling of the sublime (*CJ*, §29, 265)—to engage in the futile task of attempting to estimate aesthetically the extent of space; and this is not something that any observer is under a reasonable requirement to do.

Kant's position is rendered even less compelling by an additional twist to the line of thought I have sketched. For Kant maintains that our ability to think the [given] infinite as *a whole*—the ability to comprehend the infinite in the world of sense completely under a concept—which is not possible by means of a standard of sense (an aesthetic unit of measure), is possible only because we possess a supersensible faculty or power with its idea of a noumenon as the substrate underlying the phenomenal world. This power Kant immediately equates with 'the power of being able to think the infinite of supersensible intuition as given (in its intelligible substrate)' (*CJ*, 255),[8] this power being great beyond any comparison, i.e. absolutely great, as an expansion of the mind that from the practical point of view feels itself able to pass beyond the bounds of sensibility. Accordingly, sublimity attaches only to the supersensible basis of human nature, the apprehension of a natural phenomenon serving only as a suitable occasion for becoming conscious of this basis (*CJ*, 280). Here at last, if not earlier, it becomes clear that Kant's opening definition of the mathematically sublime as the absolutely great, which necessitates the introduction of the idea of infinity into Kant's account, and which was designed to secure the moralized conception of the sublime that Kant favoured, led to distortions (and unclarities) in Kant's elucidation of the mathematically sublime in terms of the aesthetic estimation of magnitude. These distortions usher in the infinite as something that, although given to us in our spatial experience, cannot be estimated aesthetically, but can be thought as a whole. It can be thought as a whole, as an absolute totality,[9] as unconditioned, however, only by conceiving of the sensible world of appearance as being dependent on its intelligible basis, the world as it is in itself, thus making manifest our possession of a mental power superior to sensibility, in which our status

[8] The concept of infinity appears here to be misapplied to the noumenal substrate of the phenomenal world.

[9] This picks up the first difference between the beautiful and the sublime that Kant identifies in his opening discussion of the sublime: whereas the beautiful, being focused on an object's form, is concerned with what is bounded, the sublime is concerned with boundlessness—boundlessness to which the thought of its totality is added (*CJ*, §23, 244).

as a *causa noumenon* is disclosed, the felt awareness of our supreme value as a moral agent sending a profound thrill through us.[10]

2.16.   THE DYNAMICALLY SUBLIME

Kant's account of the dynamically sublime is, on the face of it, much more straightforward. He defines the dynamically sublime in nature—exhibited by the power of a hurricane, a tidal wave, an erupting volcano, a bolt of lightning, the tumultuous ocean, the high waterfall of a mighty river, for example—as a might (a power that is superior to great obstacles) that is not considered superior to oneself. But in fact this definition needs to be understood in a relativized fashion, for Kant distinguishes two powers of resistance that each of us possesses, and the dynamically sublime must be able to overcome one of these (no matter how hard we resist), and so be superior to it, but unable to overcome the other (unless we allow it to), and so be inferior to it. The first is our physical power, which is puny in comparison with the might of certain natural phenomena, whose force is such as to overwhelm and destroy us: in the face of such might we would be helpless. So with respect to physical force, nature is overwhelmingly superior to us. The second is the ability not to abandon our moral principles and commitment to morality, even under the greatest pressure. With respect to this, nature exerts no dominance over us, for we are capable of regarding all worldly goods, our health, and even our life as being less valuable than our being a morally good person, a person with a good will, i.e. as being small in comparison with moral worth. Since we must aspire to being morally good, as persons or moral agents we must consider ourselves as being superior to nature. In short, we are subject to nature's might with respect to our self-preservation as physical beings ('natural' beings), but not as moral beings, because in so far as we are persons we must regard all physical goods, our life included, as of no consequence in comparison with our possession of a good will.

To judge nature as being dynamically sublime it must be thought of as something that we would be physically unable to

[10] In Kant's rather extravagant formulation: 'the thrill that comes over us at the mere idea of the sublime' (Kant 1974: 33).

resist the might of, and so as fearful, an object to fear. However, at the time we make such a judgement we must not actually be afraid of, be feeling fear at, what we judge to be sublime: in fact, we must consider ourselves to be safe from its might, so that there is no reason to be afraid. But these are not the only conditions Kant imposes on a judgement of the dynamically sublime. Although there is an additional requirement, and it is clear that this must involve the imagination, it is uncertain what it is.

One idea that can be put aside is that we must imagine ourselves morally resisting the natural phenomenon's might (although being physically overwhelmed by it). Indeed, this would make no sense. It is true that we might imagine a situation in which the only way of preserving ourselves from such force is by sacrificing our moral worth, and finding ourselves not being prepared to abandon our commitment to the morally good in order to save our life. But although Kant holds that nothing should make us sacrifice our moral worth for anything else we value, and that we judge nature aesthetically as dynamically sublime because it encourages us to realize that we would not, or would not have to, bow down before the might of nature if our highest principles were at stake and we had to choose whether to uphold or abandon them (*CJ*, §28, 262), he does not require us to imagine ourselves being in such a situation and remaining true to the requirements of morality despite the consequences of doing so.

The simplest way of introducing the imagination into the experience of the dynamically sublime in nature would be to require that we do not just see some natural phenomenon as being extraordinarily powerful, so powerful that it would overwhelm whatever pathetically inadequate attempts at resistance we might put up against its might, but that we imagine its power—we imagine the degree of its power or how powerful it is. This idea of imagining the power of a natural phenomenon could be understood in a number of ways, but one possibility is to interpret Kant as intending the task of the imagination in the mathematically sublime to be taken as the guide to its role in the dynamically sublime. This would mean that its task in the dynamically sublime would be to imagine a unit of power or force adequate to estimating aesthetically the might of nature's stupendous forces. But although Kant in places writes as though this is what he has in mind,[11] he does not elucidate the experience of the dynamically sublime in such a way that it is linked with the aim of estimating, without measuring instruments, how powerful a given natural phenomenon is, and there is no indication of what the nature of such a process of estimation might be. Now there would be no insuperable problem in attributing to Kant the idea that in being impressed by nature's might we form an aesthetic estimate of its power, if this means an estimate based on unaided observation of its appearance. For when we encounter some strikingly powerful natural phenomenon, we often form an impression, some kind of estimate, of the magnitude of its power merely on the basis of sight (and also, often, sound). Of course, if we were to attempt to form a precise estimate, we would undoubtedly fail. However, the fact is not that we strive to form such an estimate, only to be defeated, but that we do not even try; for in the experience of the dynamically sublime we are concerned only with the natural phenomenon's being immensely more powerful than we are, not with just how much more powerful it is. Moreover, it is entirely unclear in what sense the basis of such an estimate could be an *aesthetic* unit of measure, comprehended by the imagination, as Kant requires. Furthermore, if it were Kant's intention that his accounts of the mathematically and dynamically sublime should be unified in this way, it would be even more difficult to effect a plausible introduction of the infinite into the estimation of the dynamically sublime than it is in the estimation of the mathematically sublime. For Kant would need the infinity of nature's power to be given in our experience of nature, just as he conceives of infinity as being given in our experience of a spatial magnitude. Finally, Kant does not need to introduce the imagination into the experience of the dynamically sublime in the suggested manner—as attempting to comprehend an adequate unit of measure for an aesthetic estimation of the magnitude of nature's power—in order to secure a connection with moral-

---

[11] Kant assimilates the work of the imagination in the experience of the dynamically sublime to that of its futile task in the experience of the mathematically sublime in these two passages: 'if we expand our empirical power of representation (mathematically or dynamically) in intuiting nature, reason, as the capacity to [think] the independence of the absolute totality, inevitably intervenes and calls forth the effort of the mind, although a futile one, to make the representation of the senses adequate to this totality'; 'But this idea [of the supersensible] is awakened in us by an object the aesthetic estimation of which strains the imagination to its utmost, whether in respect of extension (mathematically) or might over the mind (dynamically)' (*CJ*, 268).

ity, since this connection has already been effected in a much more straightforward manner.

Another possibility, a hint of which might be discerned in Kant's text (*CJ*, 269), is that in addition to thinking of some natural phenomenon as something we would be unable to resist the might of, and so as fearful, we must imagine ourselves being afraid. If this were Kant's intention, perhaps the idea would be that we imagine the phenomenon's irresistible might by imagining what it would be like to be threatened by, even subjected to, its enormous power and by this means we imagine ourselves into a state of fear, experiencing fear of nature, not really, but in the imagination. Accordingly, if Kant were to think of the imaginative experience of fear as having the same hedonic sign as the real experience, the imagination would figure in the experience of the dynamically sublime in a manner that adversely affects our state of well-being, albeit only for a short time. And Kant certainly needs something of this kind if he is to remain true to his idea that the feeling of the sublime is a pleasure that arises only indirectly, from 'a momentary inhibition of the vital forces' (*CJ*, §23, 245).

But, as I have indicated, there is little, if any, textual support for this suggestion, which would in any case make the role played by the imagination in the generation of the experience of the dynamically sublime markedly less significant than its role in the experience of the mathematically sublime. Whereas in the experience of the mathematically sublime the futile striving of the imagination to encompass an adequate unit of measure for the aesthetic estimation of nature's magnitude is intimately related to the positive fruit of the experience, the feeling of our possession of a superior power, a feeling that is available to us, Kant claims (*CJ*, 258–9), only through the preceding experience of the imagination's inadequacy, in the experience of the dynamically sublime the imagination would serve only to endow the experience with the element of pain (a *frisson* of distress experienced imaginatively) demanded by Kant's double-aspect conception of the experience of the sublime.

2.17. THE DOUBLE-ASPECT EMOTION OF THE SUBLIME

What exactly does Kant take the feeling of the sublime in front of nature to be? He conceives of it as an emotion with a complex phenomenology, possessing both a twofold hedonic reaction and a twofold thought-content, the two hedonic reactions having opposite signs, the negative leading to the positive, the first involving repulsion from the perceived object, the second attraction to it. For Kant, an emotion is a feeling in which pleasure is brought about only by means of a momentary check to the vital forces within the body followed by a stronger outpouring of them (*CJ*, §14, 226), furtherance of the vital forces occasioning a feeling of well-being, hindrance the reverse. The negative component of the feeling of the sublime is an unpleasant awareness of the inadequacy of our sensory or physical power: the inadequacy of our sensory power to the perceptual comprehension of nature's immensity—our inability to construct an adequate aesthetic unit of measure, one that can be taken in in one intuition and is suitable for an estimation of the infinite—or the inadequacy of our physical power to resist the immense force of a natural object or phenomenon. The felt realization of this inadequacy, which is somewhat distressing, is forced upon us by confrontation with an appropriate natural phenomenon. The positive component is a feeling of elevation in judging our own worth, a feeling of our supremacy over the natural world, the compensatory realization that, in comparison with anything in the sensible world, however immense, even the entirety of the sensible world, and despite our physical vulnerability to the might of natural phenomena, 'the rational vocation of our cognitive powers' (*CJ*, §27, 257) and the presence within us of the moral law that commands allegiance notwithstanding obstacles of sensibility, endow us with an importance, a value, infinitely superior to that of nature.[12]

---

[12] Kant attempts to characterize the feeling of the sublime in a unitary fashion in terms of the imagination in the following way (*CJ*, 269): In its empirical use, the imagination renders our feeling of well-being dependent on our physical state, on what is 'nature' within us, and so as dependent on nature outside us. But the imagination is also an instrument of reason, and as such allows us to regard ourselves as being independent of and superior to nature. In the experience of the sublime, imagination in its first role feels sacrificed (to reason), so that there is a momentary inhibition of our feeling of well-being, with a consequent repulsion from the object, but in its second role is more than adequately compensated, receiving an expansion and a might greater than the one it has sacrificed, so that the inhibition is followed immediately by a very powerful feeling of well-being, made all the stronger because of the previous momentary check, with a consequent attraction to the object. Parts of this characterization appear better suited to Kant's account of the mathematically than the dynamically sublime, others the reverse.

But the two components of Kant's characterization of the feeling of the sublime in nature are of unequal merit. If we acknowledge Kant's restriction to pure aesthetic judgements of the sublime in nature, which concern only mere magnitude or power, and we agree that there is a distinctive double-aspect experience associated with such a judgement, one element of Kant's characterization is, I believe, to some extent plausible, but the other is wide of the mark.

The plausible idea, if not in the precise form that Kant outlines, is that of our being painfully affected by the immensity of what we face—by nature's awesome magnitude or power (or both)—when we imaginatively realize its extent or force. But, first, rather than identifying this pain, in the experience of the mathematically sublime, as arising from the imagination's fruitless struggle to come up with an appropriate unit of measure for an aesthetic estimation of nature's boundless magnitude, it would seem closer to the truth to see it as an effect on, a shock to, our everyday self-concern and self-esteem brought about by a vivid realization of our relative insignificance in the immense order of nature.[13] In fact, contrary to Kant's theory, the idea of an aesthetic estimation of magnitude does not figure at all in the analysis of the experience of the mathematically sublime, which arises from the sheer immensity of some element of nature relative to our own size, rather than from any attempt to estimate exactly or roughly how large this element is—how much larger it is than us, for example—or how large space or the universe is. Although it is true that in general we lack a sense of immense distances, a sense of how big they are, which manifests itself in our inability to imagine them, to form an adequate image or succession of images of them, Kant's theory can derive no support from this fact. For his theory is based on the idea of a failed attempt, whereas the truth is that no attempt takes place. And, second, although Kant appears not to pinpoint the exact source of this pain in the experience of the dynamically sublime, it would be plausible to identify it as arising from a heightening of the sense of our vulnerability to nature's power when we are faced by and imagine ourselves being

[13] As Kant himself recognized elsewhere: 'The ... view of a countless multitude of worlds annihilates, as it were, my importance as an animal creature, which must give back to the planet (a mere speck in the universe) the matter from which it came, the matter which is for a little time provided with vital force, we know not how' (Kant 1993: 169). Kant's awareness of this aspect of the experience of the mathematically sublime is, I believe, also recognizable in his characterization of the excessive demand made on the imagination 'as like an abyss in which it is afraid to lose itself' (*CJ*, 258).

subjected to it. In both cases, therefore, the sense of our being in the world that tends to inform the way in which we live our life is disrupted. We live our life in the only way in which a life can be lived—from the first-person point of view, with limited horizons and relative security from the natural environment. But the safe confrontation with the overpowering forces of nature is conducive to a feeling of our inadequacy to withstand them and the presence of nature's immensity is liable to induce a vivid awareness of our vanishingly small significance in the wider universe. Accordingly, the normal sense of our being in the world can be undercut either by this feeling of acute vulnerability to nature or by this realization of our minute place in nature, in either case with a disturbing effect on our emotions.[14]

The other element of Kant's account—the identification of pleasure in the sublime as pleasure in the felt realization of our superiority to nature—appears to be no more than a product of his inveterate tendency to evaluate everything by reference to moral value—by its capacity or disposition to further moral value or to make vivid morality's supreme status—a tendency that led him to moralize, in one way or another, any experience he valued. Of course, there is no reason to regard Kant as being mistaken about the nature of the positive aspect of his own emotion of the sublime. On the contrary, his reverence for morality would have led him to introduce into his own experience of great natural size or force precisely the character that his theory attributes to the pleasurable aspect of the experience of the sublime, thus enabling him to read this character off his own experience as being constitutive of the positive aspect of the experience of the sublime in general. But what was, I believe, undoubtedly a feature of Kant's own experience is highly likely to be absent from the experience of many, if not most, of us.

If, however, the invigorating, pleasurable, effect of the experience of vastness or overwhelming power in the experience of the sublime is not captured by Kant's moralizing interpretation, what explains it? If the characterizations I have offered of the negative, deflating component are on the right lines, the natural suggestion, which

[14] This is, of course, reminiscent of Schopenhauer's theory of aesthetic experience (Schopenhauer 1966: i. §39). In fact, his impressive account of the feeling of the sublime is, I believe, marred only by the intrusion of his doctrine that 'the world is my representation' and attendant conceptions—a significant intrusion, since it is the foundation of his explanation of the positive, exaltatory character of the experience.

effects a desirable unification of the experience of the sublime, is that the positive component is also a function of the disruption of our ordinary sense of self, the sudden shock of a change of vision. With the sudden dropping away, when confronted by the magnitude or power of nature, of our everyday sense of the importance of our self and its numerous concerns and projects, or of our normal sense of the security of our body from external natural forces, the heightened awareness of our manifest vulnerability and insignificance in the natural world counteracting our normal self-centredness, in the experience of the sublime the disappearance of our preoccupation with and concern for self is, after the initial shock, experienced with pleasure. And conceiving of the negative and positive elements as in this way arising from the same root has the advantage of providing an explanation of a further feature of Kant's account. For Kant conceives of the feeling of the sublime in front of nature as not just an emotion with two aspects, but as one in which there is a movement back and forth between the two aspects, an oscillation between repulsion from and attraction to the object.[15] This is precisely what would be expected to happen in any somewhat protracted observation of an awesome natural magnitude or power, if the experience of the sublime answers to the characterization I have offered.[16] In fact, Kant himself oscillates between two characterizations of the relation between the positive and negative hedonic aspects of the emotion, one representing them as being experienced concurrently (*CJ*, 257), the other as succeeding one another (*CJ*, 247, 258). These characterizations could be reconciled by construing the 'movement' from one aspect to another not as the replacement of the one by the other, but as a change in the relative prominence or salience of the aspects: neither disappears; rather, they take turns in occupying the foreground of consciousness, the one receding as the other advances. Whether or not such a reconciliation is desirable, the frequency of the need to return to the negative side in order to continue to experience the positive side varies from person to person. For the awareness, vivid or subliminal, of our cosmic insignificance and

[15] At *CJ*, 258 Kant says that the movement of the mind *especially in its inception* may be compared to a vibration.

[16] My characterization is not intended to capture the aesthetic experience evoked by certain supposedly paradigmatic objects of sublime experience, such as mountains. For there is no such thing: all such objects offer a variety of aesthetic experiences, most of which lack the particular double-aspect emotion that interests me. (For a brief history of aesthetic responses to mountains see Tuan 1990: 70–4.)

vulnerability to natural forces plays different roles in people's lives, and we differ in the ability and perparedness to realize this fact imaginatively.[17]

2.18. THE PURITY OF AESTHETIC JUDGEMENTS OF SUBLIMITY

Finally, there is a problem with Kant's account of pure aesthetic judgements about the sublimity of natural objects that arises from the stringency of his requirement of purity. Judgements about the sublimity of natural objects (or, rather, their suitability to induce a feeling of sublimity in humanity), if they are to be pure aesthetic judgements, must not be based on concepts, in particular concepts of the purposes of natural objects, purposes they have in nature (or purposes to which they can be put). Kant represents a pure aesthetic judgement of the sublime in nature as being a judgement occasioned by the boundlessness, the immensity, of matter, in its extent (the mathematically sublime) or power (the dynamically sublime), as this matter appears in perception (independently of how it is conceptualized). A pure aesthetic judgement about the mathematically sublime must consider nature merely as involving magnitude, and one about the dynamically sublime must consider nature merely as force, in both cases the judgement resting only on how nature immediately manifests itself to the eye. In other words, pure aesthetic judgements about the sublimity of nature must be based on the intrinsic character of a natural object's or phenomenon's sensible intuition or image—how the imagination, not the understanding, presents it: in

[17] Kant's characterization of the sublime elsewhere is of little help: 'The sublime (*sublime*) is that *greatness* in size or intensity which inspires awe (*magnitudo reverenda*): it simultaneously invites us to approach it (so as to make our forces equal to it) and deters us by the fear that in comparison with it we shall shrink into insignificance in our own estimation (thunder over our head, for example, or a high, rugged mountain). When we are in a safe place, the gathering of our forces to grasp the appearance, along with our anxiety about not being able to rise to its greatness, arouses *astonishment* (a feeling that is agreeable because it continuously triumphs over pain)' (Kant 1974: §68). (Compare: 'At the sight of mountains ascending to heaven, deep ravines with raging streams in them, deep-shadowed wastelands that invite melancholy meditations, and similar phenomena, a spectator [who knows he is safe] is seized by *astonishment* bordering on terror, by dread and a sacred thrill' (*CJ*, 269).)

Kant's terminology, as it is presented in the representation by which it is given, not by which it is thought. Accordingly:

> when we call the sight of the starry sky *sublime*, we must not base our judgement upon any concepts of worlds inhabited by rational beings, with the bright dots that we see filling the space above us as their suns moving in orbits prescribed for them with great purposiveness. But we must take it just as we see it, as a vast all-embracing vault; and only under such a representation may we posit the sublimity that a pure aesthetic judgement attributes to this object. Similarly, when we judge the sight of the ocean, we must not regard it as we, endowed with all kinds of knowledge (not contained, however, in the immediate intuition), *think* it, as, say, a vast realm of aquatic creatures, or as the great reservoir that supplies the water for the vapours that fill the air with clouds for the benefit of the land, or again as an element that divides continent from continent yet makes possible the greatest communication between them. Instead, to judge the ocean sublime we must regard it as the poets do, merely as it manifests itself to the eye: if it is calm, as a clear mirror of water bounded only by the heavens; if it is turbulent, as an abyss threatening to overwhelm everything. (*CJ*, 270)[18]

Here Kant rightly deems various thoughts about suitable objects of a judgement of sublimity as being irrelevant to such a judgement. But when we look at the stars, what are they given to us as? How are they immediately presented in intuition? Certainly not as very distant suns. Merely as specks of light, then? Or perhaps as distant light-emanating objects of some kind? It seems clear that only the second alternative is suited to the experience of the sublime, but this conception of what is given to us in the perception of the night sky studded with stars is not licensed by Kant's restriction of a pure aesthetic judgement about the sublime in nature to the character of the subject's sensible intuition. Kant's category of the mathematically sublime concerns spatial magnitude.[19] But neither the size nor the distance of stars can be seen: stars are presented in the visual field as spots of light, and although this is the sensible appearance of extraordinarily

---

[18] In fact, Kant introduces this passage (from the 'General Remark on the Exposition of Aesthetic Reflective Judgements') by asserting that, because he is at this stage of his argument concerned solely with pure aesthetic judgements, no examples of sublime objects of nature *that presuppose the concept of a purpose* must be chosen. But, as is evident in the passage, and is required by his strongest conception of a pure aesthetic judgement, his restriction is more severe than this.

[19] The sheer magnitude of the number of specks of light visible in the clear night sky is not to the point (as the number of grains of sand on a beach demonstrates). Rather, it is the fact that these specks of light are stars, massive, light-emitting, incredibly distant objects—distant both from ourselves and from one another.

distant, massive light-producing objects, we know this not in virtue of the intrinsic nature of the appearance. Accordingly, to respond to the appearance of the starry sky at night as the appearance of a magnitude of extraordinarily distant gigantic objects (suns) is to respond not to the bare sensible intuition of them, but under a concept of the kind of thing they are; and it is not the mere sensible appearance of the night sky, but the thought of the immensity of the universe— the immensity of the distance from us of what we can see, the immensity of the volume of space that surrounds us, and perhaps the immensity of past time (especially as exemplified by the immensity of the time taken by the light emitted from the stars to reach us)—that is responsible for the awe that thrills us when we experience that appearance as sublime. This thought is not contained in the 'immediate intuition' of the night sky, but informs the perceptual experience only of those who have acquired an understanding of what they are looking at. And in a case of what Kant entitles the dynamically sublime, the might of which must be seen as fearful, is the power of what confronts us always or ever a feature of how the object is presented in sensible intuition, rather than in thought? Kant himself construes force not as something that is given to us by sensibility, but as something that is thought through the understanding.[20]

So in both forms of the sublime, it is often the case that in order to see some natural phenomenon as being of immense magnitude or force it is necessary to see it under a concept, and in responding to it with the feeling of the sublime we are responding to an aspect of it that is not given in immediate intuition but introduced into our experience only by means of the concept through which the phenomenon is thought. Now Kant's fundamental idea about a judgement of the sublime is that sublimity is improperly predicated of a natural object, which can, at most, be said to be suitable for arousing in the mind 'a feeling that is itself sublime' (*CJ*, §23, 246), the impropriety arising most basically from the approval expressed by a predication of sublimity. It might seem, therefore, that the required adjustment to Kant's thought is the concession that natural objects regarded under (non-purposive) concepts of the kinds they instantiate—or even (if there are any)[21] organisms of immense size or power

---

[20] For Kant, the concept of force is derivative from the concept of causality, which is not a function of sensible intuition.

[21] In Kant's classification of aesthetic judgements about nature there is no counterpart with respect to the sublime of the judgement of dependent beauty. There is

regarded under purposive concepts of the natural kinds they exemplify—are just as suitable for giving rise to the feeling of the sublime as are non-purposive natural objects that are immediately given in perception as being of immense magnitude or force; and if it is the feeling that is itself sublime,[22] sublimity can be predicated of objects of the former kinds with no greater impropriety than when predicated of the latter. But this mislocates the difficulty for Kant. The problem is not that in a judgement of the sublime natural phenomena often need to be judged under the concept of the kind they instantiate. Rather, it is that the property of a natural phenomenon that is the concern of a judgement of the sublime—immensity of space or power—is a deliverance not of sensibility, but of the understanding. It is therefore unsurprising that in Kant's most well-known passage about his favourite instance of the sublime in nature, the star-studded sky at night, he does not restrict his reaction to how the sky is given to him in perception:

Two things fill the mind with ever new and increasing wonder and awe, the oftener and the more steadily we reflect on them: the starry heavens above me and the moral law within me. I do not merely conjecture them and seek them as though obscured in darkness or in the transcendent region beyond my horizon: I see them before me, and I associate them directly with the consciousness of my own existence. The heavens begin at the place I occupy in the external world of sense, and broaden the connection in which I stand into an unbounded magnitude of worlds beyond worlds and systems of systems and into the limitless times of their periodic motion, their beginning and their duration. (Kant, 1993, 'Conclusion', 169)

good reason for the omission: the notion of qualitative perfection has no application to the likely objects of the sublime in nature (a mountain, an abyss, the ocean, the starlit sky, a massive waterfall, an exploding volcano), since they lack natural functions. And no objects with natural functions have anything like the size or power of such objects as these. (For Kant, a monstrous natural object of a purposive kind could not be qualitatively perfect: 'An object is *monstrous* if by its magnitude it defeats the purpose that constitutes its concept' (*CJ*, 253).)

[22] If pleasure in the sublime is a propositional pleasure, pleasure in our awareness of ourselves as being moral agents, who have a value that transcends that of anything else, then although a judgement of the sublime will not be based on an interest *in the natural object that occasions the awareness*, it will be based on pleasure in a fact about the world.

3
Nature, Art, Aesthetic Properties, and Aesthetic Value

I believe a leaf of grass is no less than the
   journey-work of the stars,
And the pismire is equally perfect, and a grain of sand,
   and the egg of the wren,
And the tree toad is a chef-d'oeuvre for the highest,
And the running blackberry would adorn the parlors
   of heaven ...

Walt Whitman, 'Song of Myself'

3.1. INTRODUCTION

What, if anything, is distinctive of the aesthetics of nature? That nature is its subject does not in itself distinguish it from the aesthetics of anything else, the aesthetics of art, for example, at least with respect to aesthetic appreciation. For a difference in the kinds of object amenable to aesthetic appreciation might not introduce any corresponding difference into the aesthetics of different domains. For example, the fact that the aesthetics of nature is the aesthetics *of nature* is compatible with the view that there is a unitary notion of aesthetic appreciation according to which aesthetic appreciation abstracts from what kind of thing the object of appreciation is, focusing only on an item's sensible properties and how they are structured to compose the item's perceptual form. It is also compatible with the view that the aesthetics of art is basic and the aesthetics of nature is to be elucidated in terms of it. According to the first view, the aesthetic appreciation of nature and of art are distinguished only by the different natures of their objects, neither having priority over the other. According to the second view, the aesthetic appreciation of nature consists in nature's being regarded as if it were art.

But neither of these views is correct. The first can be quickly dismissed: it operates with a conception of aesthetic appreciation manifestly inadequate not just to the appreciation of art, but also to the appreciation of nature. For (leaving nature aside) the aesthetic appreciation of works of art as works of art is appreciation of them under concepts of the kinds of works of art they are, and perceptually indistinguishable works nevertheless possess different aesthetic properties (as with appropriation art that replicates the original). The second view can also be dismissed if, as I believe,[1] just as the aesthetic appreciation of art is the appreciation of art *as art*, so the aesthetic appreciation of nature is the aesthetic appreciation of nature *as nature*. For, given that the natural world is not anyone's artefact, the aesthetic appreciation of nature as nature, if it is to be true to what nature actually is, must be the aesthetic appreciation of nature *not* as an intentionally produced object (and so not as art).

But the rejection of the view that the aesthetic appreciation of nature consists in appreciating nature as if it were art does not need to rest on the acceptance of this conception of the aesthetic appreciation of nature as nature. For two demands can be made of this view, neither of which can be met. First, the undeniable fact that it is possible to regard a natural object as if it were a work of art does not entail that this is how we do or should regard natural objects when we experience them aesthetically. So an argument is needed to bridge the gap from possibility to actuality or necessity. Second, an account of the aesthetic appreciation of nature must be true to the characteristic phenomenology of the experience of appreciating nature aesthetically.

The impossibility of meeting these two demands can be illustrated by a consideration of the best-articulated attempt to construe the aesthetic appreciation of nature on the model of the appreciation of art. Anthony Savile's account (Savile 1982: ch. 8) is superior to other versions of the view precisely because it takes seriously the implications of the idea of regarding a natural item *as if it were* a work of art, which requires integrating natural beauty into an account of artistic value. One admirable feature of Savile's account is that, although it assimilates the aesthetic appreciation of nature to the appreciation of art, it credits the aesthetics of nature with a distinctive character.

[1] See Essay 1. This conception of the aesthetic appreciation of nature has long been recognized by Allen Carlson and Holmes Rolston III, among others.

For the difference between art and nature, which must figure in any adequate aesthetics, is reflected in a feature—a kind of freedom and a correlative form of relativity—attributed to aesthetic judgements about the beauty of natural items but which is not possessed by judgements about the beauty of art. I believe that judgements of natural beauty are distinguished by a kind of freedom and a form of relativity that does not pertain to judgements of artistic value, but the versions of these ideas I favour are quite different from Savile's.

3.2. THE BEAUTY OF ART AND THE BEAUTY OF NATURE

The analysis that Savile proposes of the beauty of a work of art is based on the idea that, necessarily, every work of art answers to some problem, which means that it is constructed to fit a description indicated by its overall conception, the artist's guiding overall intention, a problem that the artist attempts to resolve within a set of aesthetic constraints that can be called a style. In essence, the idea is that a work of art is beautiful if and only if, when seen as answering to its problem in its style, it evokes the appropriate response, this appropriate response being the feeling of satisfaction we experience when we recognize that the solution a work of art proposes to its problem within its aesthetic constraints is just right.

But if 'beauty' is, as Savile maintains, the most general term of aesthetic praise, univocal, whether predicated of art or nature, the analysis must be extendable to cover cases of natural as well as artistic beauty without importing an ambiguity into the concept of beauty. Now although the notions of problem and style have no place in nature, this does not preclude the possibility of regarding a natural object as if it were a work of art constructed as the solution to a certain problem within a set of stylistic constraints. And if this is the way in which we do or must experience natural beauty, the fact that there is no place in nature for style and problem is no obstacle to a unitary account of beauty. But for any natural object it will always be possible to think of some style and problem which are such that the object can be seen as a satisfactory solution to that problem within the aesthetic constraints of that style, so that each natural object will be beautiful under one description or another. Accordingly, Savile amends his account of beauty so that a judgement of something's beauty is a judgement of it *under* a description (a problem) and a style, so that the truth-value of a judgement of a natural object's beauty is relative to the description and style chosen by the beholder, who is free (unlike the beholder of a work of art) to select whatever description and style he or she likes.

But this is not sufficient to overcome the problem that natural beauty poses for the account. For possibility is not the same as actuality or necessity: the fact that it is possible to regard a natural object as if it were a work of art does not entail that this is how we do or should regard natural objects when we experience them as being beautiful. To bridge the gap between possibility and actuality/necessity, Savile first insists that judging something as if it were a work of art (when it is not) is not a mere possibility, but something that on occasion actually happens (with a detail of a work of art). Then:

To make it plausible that this is what happens in the natural case too we have only to find an explanation of the point of doing so [i.e. of judging a natural object as if it were a work of art]. We have, that is, to explain why we should care that *nature* exhibits beauty. (Savile 1982: 181–2)

Savile suggests (along Kantian lines, although operating with a different conception of beauty) that there is good reason to experience natural things as being beautiful. For in doing so we love them; in loving nature our integration in the world is encouraged; 'such attachments to the world as are furthered through the appreciation of its beauties encourage reverence for it and a respect for the claims that it makes against ourselves' (Savile 1982: 182); and so, in loving something disinterestedly that is distinct from ourselves, morality is furthered.

But this explanation of why we should care that nature exhibits beauty, whatever its merits, fails to bridge the gap in the argument. For what is needed is (i) an explanation of the point of judging a natural object as if it were a work of art, and (ii) an argument to the effect that this mode of judgement is mandatory or the only possibility for the judgement of natural beauty. And the suggestion fails to address (ii). Furthermore, the gap in the argument is, I believe, unbridgeable. For, first, it is not impossible to see the natural world aesthetically except by seeing it as if it were art. Second, it is untrue that, unless nature is seen as if it were art, there is little of aesthetic interest in nature. Third, the Kantian considerations that postulate a link between the experience of natural things as being beautiful and the furtherance of morality are as readily available to the aesthetic appreciation of nature as what nature actually is. Indeed, they are more naturally available to this conception. For only so does nature actually *exhibit* beauty and the question arise as to the importance of our caring that it does. If we regard nature as if it were what we know it not to be, and are free to select problem and style as we choose, so that with enough imagination we can see anything as beautiful (or, instead, as lacking beauty), we have no reason to care what nature is actually like and so no reason to love it for what it is. And, finally, the experience of nature as if it were art offers no benefits substantial enough to outweigh the advantages of the aesthetic experience of nature as what it actually is, so that it would be better to experience it in the first rather than the second manner. Accordingly, it is not mandatory to judge a natural item aesthetically as if it were a work of art; and given that nature is not art, to judge it as if it were art is to misjudge it.

Now any version of the claim that the aesthetic appreciation of nature consists in nature's being regarded as if it were art must, whatever conception of artistic value it embraces, represent the aesthetic appreciation of nature as being informed by concepts integral to artistic appreciation but which are known not to be applicable to nature. It therefore faces the same insuperable obstacle presented to Savile's account of aesthetic judgements of natural beauty. Furthermore, it will be vulnerable to a crucial objection— one that I have not yet brought against Savile's version[2]—namely, that it is untrue to the phenomenology of the aesthetic experience of nature. For the aesthetic experience of nature is not impregnated with those notions essential to the appreciation of art: the satisfaction we experience when we find a tree, a bird, a landscape or skyscape beautiful is not that of seeing an object as an excellent solution to a problem within a set of aesthetic constraints constitutive of a style, nor does it answer to any viable alternative conception of artistic value. On the contrary, the (non-theistic) aesthetic appreciation of nature is saturated with an unbracketed consciousness, clear or dim, of nature's not being art.

---

[2] I leave aside Savile's commitment to the view that 'beautiful' is always used as an attributive adjective, never predicatively. The reason he gives in support of this view is that an item can be beautiful as an F and yet not beautiful as a G. But this does not imply that 'beautiful' is never used predicatively. See Frank Sibley's (2001a) for the definitive treatment of the issue.

3.3. APPRECIATING NATURE AS WHAT NATURE ACTUALLY IS

Given the unacceptability of the view that the aesthetic appreciation of natural items should be thought of as the appreciation of them under concepts of art, the obvious alternative is that they should be appreciated under concepts of the natural things or phenomena that they are. And this alternative conception of the aesthetic appreciation of natural items will have a special aesthetic significance in so far as two theses of Kendall Walton (Walton 1970) about the connection between the aesthetic properties of works of art and the categories of art to which they belong hold equally for the connection between the aesthetic properties of natural items and categories of nature. Applied to nature these theses become: (i) (the psychological thesis) What aesthetic properties a natural item *appears* to possess—what aesthetic properties the item is perceived or experienced as possessing—is a function of the category or categories of nature under which it is experienced (i.e. what sort of natural thing it is perceived as being); and (ii) (the philosophical thesis) What aesthetic properties the item *really* possesses is determined by the right categories of nature to experience the item as falling under—it really possesses those aesthetic properties it appears to possess when perceived in its *correct* categories of nature (by an aesthetically sensitive and properly informed observer who employs the relevant knowledge of what items in that category are standardly like to so perceive it).

But it is compatible with the requirement that the aesthetic appreciation of nature is the aesthetic appreciation of nature as nature (as what nature actually is) that natural items should be appreciated aesthetically under no concepts at all (except that of nature itself); that is, not as instances of the kinds they exemplify, but only with respect to their sensible qualities, the way in which they compose their items' perceptual forms, and the aesthetic properties they possess in virtue of these qualities and forms.[3] Now although we

[3] As Allen Carlson has argued (Carlson 1979*b*), it is only a framed view of the natural environment, not the environment itself, that possesses formal qualities, although I am unpersuaded by the stronger claim he favours, that, *when appreciated aesthetically in the appropriate mode*, it is not possible to see a section of it as having any formal qualities. See Essay 4, §3. But, in any case, what is true of the aesthetic appreciation of the natural environment is not thereby true of the aesthetic appreciation of nature.

rarely, if ever, aesthetically appreciate a natural item merely as being natural, and to do so would be to engage in a diminished form of aesthetic appreciation of nature, we often delight aesthetically in natural items that we perceive only under highly general concepts (*flower*), not as instances of the specific kinds they exemplify (*orchid*), or under one concept (*flower*), but not another coextensive concept that expresses a deeper understanding of the nature or function of the kind (*sexual organ of plant*). This brings out a lack of clarity in the idea of appreciating a natural thing as the natural thing it is, for any natural thing falls under more or less specific concepts of nature, and can be appreciated under concepts that express a greater or lesser understanding of it. And it also brings out a problem for Walton's philosophical thesis transferred to nature.[4] The problem is: What determines which concept or concepts of nature are the correct concept or concepts under which a natural item is to be perceived? For what is at issue is not just whether a natural item falls under a certain concept of nature, but which of those concepts it falls under it should be perceived under *from the aesthetic point of view*, where this means that perception under these concepts discloses the aesthetic properties it really possesses and thereby makes possible a proper assessment of its aesthetic value. A non-category-relative interpretation of judgements of the aesthetic properties of natural items requires that a natural thing should not fall under different concepts of nature which are such that, when perceived under these concepts—the correct concepts to perceive it under—it is properly experienced as possessing incompatible aesthetic properties. Since the same natural item falls under a variety of concepts of nature, the successful transference of the non-psychological thesis to nature stands in need of a criterion of correctness that will deliver the required result. And there is an additional difficulty about the aesthetic properties and aesthetic value of

---

[4] There is no difficulty in transferring the psychological thesis from art to nature (although I believe that, in virtue of natural items not being the products of artists, it holds only in an impoverished form): just as the perceived aesthetic character of a work is a function of which of its non-aesthetic perceptual features are 'standard', 'variable', or 'contra-standard' for one who perceives the work under a certain category of art, so the perceived aesthetic character of a natural thing is a function of which of its non-aesthetic perceptual features are standard, variable, or contra-standard for one who perceives it under a certain category of nature. See Essay 4, §6. Carlson (1981) tries to show that both the psychological and the philosophical thesis can be transferred to nature.

natural things, considered as the kinds of natural things they are, which concerns how they should be appreciated aesthetically and what is relevant to their aesthetic appreciation. For there is an important disanalogy between the constraints imposed on aesthetic appreciation by, on the one hand, the fact that an item is to be appreciated as the work of art it is, and, on the other, the fact that it is to be appreciated as the natural item it is. This difference assumes crucial significance in an assessment of the doctrine of positive aesthetics with respect to nature.

3.4. POSITIVE AESTHETICS WITH RESPECT TO NATURE

Positive aesthetics with respect to nature maintains that there is the following vital difference between the aesthetic appreciation of virgin nature and the appreciation of art (or nature affected by humanity): whereas the aesthetics of untouched nature is positive, involving only the acceptance and aesthetic appreciation of whatever exists in nature, the aesthetics of art is critical in the sense that it allows for negative aesthetic judgement. And, so positive aesthetics claims, the reason for this difference, the reason that negative aesthetic criticism is out of place in the aesthetic appreciation of nature, is that *the natural world untouched by humanity is essentially aesthetically good.*[5] But this doctrine needs to be made more precise. First, there is the question of its scope. It could be taken to apply to (i) nature taken as a whole, (ii) the earth's (or any other planet's) biosphere, (iii) each ecosystem, (iv) each kind of natural (or perhaps organic) item, (v) each particular natural (organic) thing, (vi) each natural event (or connected sequence of events). Second, there is the question of its strength. The claim that nature unmodified by humanity is essentially aesthetically good might be understood to allow that pristine nature possesses some negative aesthetic qualities (but qualities that are

---

[5] In his (1984) Allen Carlson decisively criticizes three possible justifications of positive aesthetics before presenting what he takes to be a more plausible justification of the doctrine. This is the first of the arguments I examine below. Stan Godlovitch distinguishes and examines various interpretations of positive aesthetics in his (1998a). Note that, taken strictly, nature unaffected by humanity now includes relatively little, if anything, within the biosphere.

always 'outweighed' by positive aesthetic qualities), or might be intended to rule out this possibility.[6] Since it would not be enough to claim that every natural item has some aesthetically valuable quality or qualities—a claim that would appear to be almost as plausible for artefacts as for nature—then, leaving nature taken as a whole aside, positive aesthetics must claim that each biosphere, ecosystem, kind of natural item, particular natural thing, or natural occurrence (a) lacks negative and possesses positive aesthetic qualities, (b) has positive aesthetic value *overall* or *on balance*, or (c) has *equal* overall positive aesthetic value.[7] Third, there is the question of the doctrine's modal status. Is it supposed to be some kind of necessary truth about nature or might nature have been otherwise?

Two arguments put forward by Allen Carlson in support of positive aesthetics, neither of which uses as a premise that any individual natural items have a positive aesthetic value, deserve examination. The first (Carlson 1984) runs as follows. In order to appreciate what aesthetic qualities and aesthetic value an item has it is necessary to know how it is to be perceived, which requires knowledge of what kind of thing it is. What aesthetic qualities something possesses are those it appears to possess when perceived in its correct category. The correct categories for the aesthetic appreciation of nature—natural objects and landscapes, for example—are those provided and informed by natural science. So positive aesthetics will be established if, and only if, it can be shown that the natural world (unaffected by humanity) must seem aesthetically good when perceived in categories of nature (under which it falls): the aesthetic qualities of nature are those it appears to have when appropriately aesthetically appreciated, i.e. when perceived under its correct categories, categories of nature; and so nature is essentially aesthetically good if, and only if, this is how it appears when perceived in those

[6] The second alternative is embraced by Eugene Hargrove (1989: 177): 'nature is beautiful and has no negative aesthetic qualities', quoted in Godlovitch (1998a). Whether or not nature lacks negative aesthetic qualities, it is immune to all the many defects to which art is liable in virtue of being the product of intelligent design.

[7] Note that the view that each natural thing (ecosystem, or whatever) has equal positive overall aesthetic value (i) is non-commital about the *degree* of that value, which, for all it claims, might be rather low, and (ii) denies that issues of the comparative aesthetic values of natural items are ever *indeterminate*—that it is neither true that one of the items has a greater aesthetic value than the other nor that they are precisely equal in value. But it would be charitable to interpret 'equal' as meaning 'roughly equal', in which case indeterminacy is allowed, perhaps inevitable (unless the items are of the same kind and indiscernible).

categories of nature it belongs to. This will be so if the categories created by science for landscapes and natural objects are such that the correctness of these categories is determined by the criterion of aesthetic goodness; that is, if the correct categories are those that are such that nature seems aesthetically good when perceived in them. But 'aesthetic goodness is certainly not *the* criterion by which scientists determine correctness of descriptions, categories, and theories' (Carlson 1984: 30). However, the creation of categories of nature and their correctness are in an important sense dependent on aesthetic considerations. For:

a more correct categorization in science is one that over time makes the natural world seem more intelligible, more comprehensible to those whose science it is. Our science appeals to certain kinds of qualities to accomplish this. These qualities are ones such as order, regularity, harmony, balance, tension, conflict, resolution, and so forth. If our science did not discover, uncover, or create such qualities in the natural world and explain that world in terms of them, it would not accomplish its task of making it seem more intelligible to us; rather, it would leave the world incomprehensible, as any of the various world views which we regard as superstition seem to us to leave it. Moreover, these qualities which make the world seem comprehensible to us are also those which we find aesthetically good. Thus, when we experience them in the natural world or experience the natural world in terms of them, we find it aesthetically good. (Carlson 1984: 30–1)

In short: Since the categories of nature created by science are the correct categories in which to appreciate it, and since these categories are created partly in light of aesthetic goodness and so make the natural world appear aesthetically good when perceived in these categories, the natural world is aesthetically good. And this position, Carlson argues, receives support from the fact that advances in science are closely correlated with developments in the aesthetic appreciation of nature. For example, the positive aesthetic appreciation of, on the one hand, previously abhorred landscapes, such as mountains and jungles, and, on the other, previously abhorred life forms, such as insects and reptiles, seems to have followed developments in geology and geography, and in biology, respectively.

The second argument (Carlson 1993) maintains that the appreciation of nature should be understood as a form of 'order appreciation'. Order appreciation consists in a selection of objects to be appreciated and a focusing on a certain kind of order that the objects display. The focus is on the order imposed on the selected objects by the various forces, random or otherwise, which produce these objects. 'Order' means 'ordered pattern—a pattern ordered by and revelatory of the forces of creation or selection responsible for it'. The selection is by reference to a general non-aesthetic and non-artistic account which, by making this order manifest and intelligible, makes the objects appreciable. In the case of nature, (i) the relevant order is the natural order, (ii) the relevant forces are the geological, biological, and meteorological forces which produce the natural order, and (iii) the relevant account is that given by natural science—astronomy, physics, chemistry, biology, meteorology, and geology. And because all of nature necessarily reveals the natural order, all natural objects are (more or less) 'equally appreciable', 'equally aesthetically appealing', 'equal in beauty and importance', so that 'selection among all that the natural world offers is not of much ultimate importance'.

Now it is unclear exactly which version of positive aesthetics these arguments are intended to establish. If the scope is not just kinds but also instances of them,[8] and the doctrine is that all natural things have *equal* positive aesthetic value,[9] the arguments are unconvincing. Consider (the selection of) a single living natural object—a plant or animal, for example. There is nothing in the second argument to prevent the conclusion that each natural object is equally aesthetically appealing from meaning that each organic natural object, *at each moment of its life*, is equally aesthetically appealing. But the fact that a living object's condition, which might be diseased or malformed or indicative of approaching death, is explicable in terms of natural forces and processes does not entail that, when seen as the product of such forces, the object, in that condition, must or should be seen as just as equally aesthetically appealing as any other natural object, or as itself in any of its former or later conditions. On the contrary, living objects decline, are subject to illness or lack of

---

[8] Carlson is inclined to believe that the justification of positive aesthetics offered in the first argument makes the thesis applicable not just to kinds but also to instances of them: 'given the role of aesthetic goodness in scientific description, categorization, and theorizing, I suspect that scientific knowledge as a whole is aesthetically imbued such that our appreciation of particulars is as enhanced as is that of kinds' (Carlson 1984: 32 n. 67).

[9] That this is Carlson's position in Carlson (1984) is confirmed by endnote 61 of Carlson (1993), which refers the reader to Carlson (1984) for a fuller development of the line of thought leading to the conclusion that 'natural objects all seem equally aesthetically appealing' (Carlson 1993: 222).

nutrients that affect their appearance, lose their attractive colours and (if they possess the power of locomotion) whatever ease and gracefulness of movement they formerly possessed, and in so doing diminish in aesthetic appeal. Any argument that yields the conclusion that each living natural object is equally aesthetically appealing at each stage of its life and is as aesthetically appealing as any other natural object must be defective. And the two arguments, understood as aimed at the conclusion that each particular natural thing has a roughly equal positive overall aesthetic value, are unsound.

The first argument concludes from the fact that (positive) aesthetic considerations partly determine the categories created by science to render the natural world intelligible, which are the correct categories in which to perceive nature, that the natural world is aesthetically good. But this summary statement blurs an essential feature of the argument, which is that science accomplishes its task of rendering the natural world intelligible by discovering positive aesthetic qualities in nature. Accordingly, 'when we experience them in the natural world or experience the natural world in terms of them, we find it aesthetically good'. These qualities are ones 'such as order, regularity, harmony, balance, tension, conflict, and resolution', which are the kinds of qualities we find good in art. Now it is unclear how the final three qualities contribute to the argument. Neither tension nor conflict is in itself a positive aesthetic quality and the resolution of tension or conflict, whether in art or nature, might come about in a manner that is not, from the aesthetic point of view, attractive. Furthermore, the aesthetic appreciation of a natural item need not be impregnated with the concepts of tension, conflict, and resolution on pain of being shallow or in some other way defective, for it is often the case that a natural thing is not in a state of tension or conflict (in any ordinary sense). Accordingly, appeal to such qualities as these could not bear the weight of the argument. As for the first three qualities, they seem to be little more than reflections of the law-governed character of nature, and it does not follow from the fact that each natural thing, and each part of it, is subject to natural law that all natural objects are equally aesthetically appealing.[10] Even if some aesthetic appeal accrues to an item in virtue of being law-governed, natural objects will nevertheless vary

[10] Note that simplicity and elegance, for example, which are desired qualities of theories, the second being also an aesthetic quality, are not, at least explicitly, being appealed to in the argument, although they perhaps fall under the 'such as'.

in their aesthetic appeal, manifesting different positive aesthetic qualities. Moreover, being governed by law does not preclude possession of negative aesthetic qualities, nor guarantee possession, by any natural object that possesses negative aesthetic qualities, of compensating positive aesthetic qualities such that each natural object has the same overall aesthetic value. And grossly malformed living things will remain grotesque no matter how comprehensible science renders their malformation.

Putting aside the issue whether the correct model for the appreciation of nature is order appreciation, the second argument, which as it stands contains no reference to aesthetic qualities figuring in the determination of categories of nature, fares no better—perhaps worse. It may be true that, from the point of view of the appreciation of nature, there is an enormous, perhaps an infinite, amount to be understood about what composes any natural thing and how it was generated by the forces and materials of nature, but this implies nothing about the *aesthetic* qualities of the item—in particular, that these are essentially positive and equal in value to those of anything else in nature. The fact that the order imposed on any selected natural objects by the various forces that produced them is the natural order, so that 'all of nature necessarily reveals the natural order', does not imply that the order manifest in any selection from nature is, from the aesthetic point of view, equally attractive, interesting, or valuable. Not all appreciation is aesthetic appreciation, and the argument, as it stands, slides from 'equally appreciable', meaning 'equally displaying the natural order', to 'equally appreciable', meaning 'equally aesthetically valuable'.

Although the rejection of the view that each natural thing, at each moment of its existence, has overall positive aesthetic value does not imply the rejection of the view that each natural thing, taken as a whole, i.e. considered throughout its duration, has overall positive aesthetic value (roughly equal to that of each natural thing), this weaker position does not recommend itself. Apart from the question how the aesthetic value of a natural item, taken as a whole, should be determined, natural items come in such various guises, biotic and non-biotic, of short or long duration, and answering to different criteria of identity, as to preclude the truth of any universal claim about their aesthetic values.

If, as seems clear, there is no hope for the most ambitious version of positive aesthetics, in what form might the doctrine be preserved?

First, its scope must be changed. It would perhaps be more plausible if it were to be a claim not about particulars, but about kinds. For each kind of living thing is endowed with some aesthetic value in virtue of possessing parts with natural functions they are well suited to perform,[11] their exercise sometimes displaying such attractive aesthetic qualities as gracefulness of movement; and many biotic kinds (all flowers, perhaps) undoubtedly possess a positive overall aesthetic value. There are even kinds of natural object (galaxy, star, ocean) or occurrence (exploding volcano) which are such that, on one understanding of the notion, each instance of them is sublime.[12] Nevertheless, on the one hand, there are many kinds of natural item that are not forms of life and whose character appears ill suited to guarantee a positive overall aesthetic value, and, on the other, perhaps there are forms of life that do not possess a positive overall aesthetic value. In any case, categories of nature exhibit such diversity—a few (*hill*) are basically morphological, some (*rainbow*) collect mere appearances, others (*nest*) are defined by the use made of them, and so on—as to render hazardous a doctrine of positive aesthetics about kinds of natural item.

What about ecosystems? The claim that any ecosystem, taken as a whole, inevitably has a positive overall aesthetic value (roughly comparable to that of any other) raises three issues, one concerning the basis of the claim, one concerning the appreciation of the postulated aesthetic value, and one concerning the relation between the aesthetic appreciation of an ecosystem and the aesthetic appreciation of items in it. If it is indeed true that each ecosystem must have a positive overall aesthetic value, this necessity must stem from the character of such a system. Now an ecosystem, in the sense at issue, is a relatively self-contained segment of nature, an integrated, self-maintaining biological community and its environment, that contains a rich variety of interdependent life forms, each with its own

---

[11] Compare Aristotle (2001, 645^{a}23–5). Burke's well-known counter examples (Burke 1958: pt. III, §VI) to the view that the beauty of natural objects derives from the fitness of their parts to their various purposes—'the wedge-like snout of a swine', 'the great bag hanging to the bill of a pelican', the prickly hide of a hedgehog and 'missile quills' of a porcupine, for instance—were perhaps well chosen to appeal to the common prejudices of the time, but in fact are not inconsistent even with his own conception of beauty (as that quality or those qualities in objects by which they cause love or some similar passion).

[12] Compare Holmes Rolston III (1998: 164): 'Like clouds, seashores, and mountains, forests are never ugly, they are only more or less beautiful; the scale runs from zero upward with no negative domain.'

niche, that is a product of selection pressures, and that involves a multiplicity of circular movements of energy within the system by means of biological processes whereby parts of one life form are assimilated by others, the parts of which are in turn assimilated by others, with at some point or points a decomposition of organic structure into elements that nourish new life taking place. It is unclear exactly how this essence is supposed to guarantee a positive overall aesthetic value, especially in the light of there being a great deal of killing and suffering in most ecosystems.

Perhaps the most plausible line of thought runs as follows: Although an ecosystem will contain objects and events that, in themselves, possess a negative aesthetic value, when these are seen in the context of the recycling of resources intrinsic to the system, which issues in the perpetual re-creation of life (much of which is beautiful):

the ugly parts do not subtract from but rather enrich the whole. The ugliness is contained, overcome, and integrates into positive, complex beauty. (Rolston III 1988: 241)

Here there appear to be four ideas: first, that many, perhaps a great majority, of the living forms in an ecosystem are in themselves beautiful; second, that any local ugliness is just a stage in a process that issues in beauty; third, that this local ugliness, when seen as a prelude to the creation of new life, is diminished; and, fourth, that in virtue of the continual creation of life by means of the biological processes at work in the system, the system, considered as the temporal unfolding of those processes, is itself beautiful (or sublime).[13] If the first of these ideas, even when combined with the vital consideration that nature is immune to all defects to which art is liable in virtue of being the product of intelligent design, is not sufficient to guarantee each ecosystem a positive aesthetic value—as it might not be, given that each living thing sooner or later becomes aesthetically unattractive in itself as it deteriorates, dies, and decomposes—the weight must be borne by the last.

But even if it could be shown that each ecosystem must have a (roughly equal) positive overall aesthetic value, there would be problems about the appreciation of that value (leaving aside the issue of the temporal and spatial limits of an ecosystem). If an ecosystem's

---

[13] See Rolston III (1988: 243–5).

having a positive overall aesthetic value is a matter of how the various events in it are related to one another, either all the events that take place within it are relevant to the determination of that value or only a subset of them is, in which case the distinguishing feature of the subset, if it is to be viable, must square with the concept of an item's aesthetic value. (Perhaps the only requirement imposed by the idea of the aesthetic is that events integral to a system's aesthetic value should be perceptible.) In either case, the fact that an observer will perceive only a small time-slice of an ecosystem, and even then only a small part of what is contained within that time-slice, presents a problem for the appreciation of the aesthetic value of that ecosystem, a problem that cannot be avoided by emphasis on the transformation of perception by knowledge, the ecologically informed observer perceiving events and states within an ecosystem *as* stages in circular movements of energy through different forms of life. For, in addition to the difficulty presented to an observer of encompassing the totality of an ecosystem in its spatial extent, the temporal duration of an ecosystem is likely to exceed, often greatly so, the time one might give to observing it, precluding the realistic possibility of one's appreciating that value, no matter how much one's perception of things or events in it might be informed by relevant ecological knowledge or how vividly one might imaginatively realize the biological processes that underlie and are responsible for the visual or other appearance of the system. In the appreciation of a temporal work of art (or a literary work) it is necessary to experience the work from beginning to end, following the way in which part succeeds part as the work unfolds: only in this way is it possible to form a judgement of its artistic success. But myriad events integral to the stability of an ecosystem take place within the system in such a manner—underground, in the dark, within a living thing—as to be normally unobservable, or beyond the limits of observation (as with the release of nutrients from humus back into the soil). Furthermore, the colours of natural things, as we human beings see them, are not integral to the maintenance and functioning of an ecosystem, yet figure prominently in our aesthetic appreciation of nature; innumerable sounds, some of which do and some of which do not play a functional role in an ecosystem, are too deep or high-pitched for us to hear; many of the smells of nature, the scents of animals, for example, escape our detection and yet are of crucial significance in the working of an ecosystem; and in general the smells, tastes, colours, sounds, and feels of an ecosystem, as perceived by humans, are different from their appearance to those creatures that inhabit the system and are capable of perceiving them, and mean nothing to those living things that cannot perceive them but form an integral part of the system.

The idea that each ecosystem (or other natural system) has a positive overall aesthetic value implies nothing about the aesthetic values of the natural items it contains considered in themselves—in particular, that these are always positive. But the aesthetic significance of such values not always being positive would be undermined if, from the aesthetic point of view, any natural item in an ecosystem should properly be considered not in itself, but in relation to the ecosystem of which it forms a part[14] (or the natural environment of its creation).[15] However, there is nothing in the notion of aesthetic appreciation that licenses this requirement: the idea of the aesthetic appreciation of nature as nature—as what nature actually is—does not imply that every natural fact about a natural item, and in particular its role in an ecosystem, is relevant to the aesthetic appreciation of that item (as being natural) and so must be taken into account if the aesthetic appreciation of that natural item is not to be defective or shallow. It is true that just as the appreciation of a work of art requires that its parts be considered aesthetically in the context of the entire work, so the aesthetic appreciation of an ecosystem requires that any natural item in it be considered aesthetically in the light of its role in that system. But this does not yield the desired conclusion, which is an unconditional, not a conditional, requirement.

3.5. FREEDOM AND RELATIVITY IN THE AESTHETIC APPRECIATION OF NATURE

What, then, is the aesthetic value of nature? I shall restrict myself to natural items, rather than sequences of events, and focus primarily

---

[14] 'Every item must be seen not in framed isolation but framed by its environment, and this frame in turn becomes part of the bigger picture we have to appreciate—not a "frame" but a dramatic play' (Rolston III 1988: 239). As Yuriko Saito points out (Saito 1998), the natural consequence of this line of thought is that the proper object of aesthetic appreciation is the entire global ecosphere (if not some larger portion of nature).

[15] A highly implausible requirement imposed on organic and inorganic items alike by Allen Carlson's natural-environment model (Carlson 1979a). See Essay 4, §9.

on vision, while recognizing that the other senses play a significant role in the aesthetic experience of nature.[16] If the aesthetic appreciation of nature is appreciation of the aesthetic properties and aesthetic value of a natural item *qua* the natural thing it is, the question is what aesthetic properties and value natural items possess. Here I need to make good a claim about the aesthetic properties and values of natural items that I made earlier but did not elaborate.

First, it is necessary to clarify Walton's thesis about the relation between the aesthetic properties of a work of art and the categories of art to which it belongs. For it is not accurately represented by the formulation that a work really possesses those aesthetic properties it appears to possess when perceived in its correct categories of art by a duly sensitive observer. This would not be sufficient because, first, the work might not be in its optimal condition, and, second, the conditions of observation might not be appropriate. Accordingly, the thesis is that a work's real aesthetic properties are those manifest to a duly sensitive and well-informed observer who perceives the work in its correct artistic categories under the right conditions at the right time.

Now one issue that a defence of positive aesthetics should engage with is that of the proper level of observation at which a natural item's aesthetic qualities are supposed to appear to the informed observer. A grain of sand, observed with the naked eye, lacks as great an aesthetic appeal as many other natural things; but a microscope enables us, if not 'To see a world in a grain of sand' (William Blake, 'Auguries of Innocence'), at least to see its microstructure (at a certain level), and this is likely to have a greater aesthetic appeal than its appearance to the naked eye. Similarly, a drop of water from a lake contains a multitude of organisms visible under a microscope, which possess aesthetic properties of various kinds and constitute a possible source of aesthetic value. Positive aesthetics with respect to nature would be more plausible if it were to maintain that each natural thing, at some level of observation, has a positive aesthetic value. But level of observation is just one of many factors that affect a natural thing's aesthetic appeal and manifest aesthetic qualities: other relevant factors include the observer's distance from the

---

[16] If aesthetic value is aesthetic value *for human beings*, various restrictions on the scope of the doctrine of positive aesthetics would be needed to avoid possible counter examples drawn from the other senses—smells or tastes that all human beings find physically nauseating, for example.

object, the observer's point of view, and the nature of the light that illuminates the object. Furthermore, not only do the appearances of natural things vary under different conditions of observation, but natural things themselves undergo changes that cause them to display different aesthetic qualities at different times and make them more or less aesthetically appealing.[17] So the manifest aesthetic qualities of a natural item are relative to conditions both of observation and time.

The transference to nature of Walton's thesis about the aesthetic properties that works of art really possess must accommodate a crucial difference between the appreciation of art and the aesthetic appreciation of nature, which is linked with a disanalogy between the way in which categories of art and categories of nature function in the determination of the aesthetic properties and value of those items that belong to them. Whereas works of art are either immutable (if they are types), or, if subject to change, standardly have an optimal condition—at least, according to the intention of their creator—in which their aesthetic properties are manifest, not only is nature always changing but it has no optimal condition in which its aesthetic properties are manifest; and whereas certain observational manners and conditions are in general either privileged or ruled out for works of art, this is not so for natural things. Categories of nature do not function to partially determine the real aesthetic properties of natural items as categories of art do those of works of art. That natural items are not designed for the purpose of aesthetic appreciation releases them from the constraints governing the artistic appreciation of works of art: categories of art prescribe the appropriate manner of artistic appreciation as categories of nature do not prescribe the appropriate manner of aesthetic appreciation of nature. The aesthetic appreciation of nature is thereby endowed with a freedom denied to artistic appreciation: in a section of the natural world we are free to frame elements as we please, to adopt any position or move in any way, at any time of the day or night, in any atmospheric conditions, and to use any sense modality, without thereby incurring the charge of misunderstanding. No visible aspect, quality, or structure of a natural item, of its exterior or interior, perceived from any direction or distance, with or without optical

---

[17] In fact, the transient character of a natural phenomenon or a natural object's power of endurance or its longevity can itself be an aspect of its aesthetic appeal.

instruments, is deemed irrelevant to the aesthetic appreciation of that item by the requirement that it must be appreciated as the kind of natural item it is. And the same is true, *mutatis mutandis*, for the other sense modalities, in so far as the perception of taste, smell, felt texture, movement, pressure, and heat falls within the bounds of the aesthetic. The fact that an object is to be appreciated as a painting means that its weight is irrelevant, as are its smell, taste, and felt warmth or coldness; but the fact that an object is to be appreciated aesthetically as a river or as a tree in itself rules out no mode of perception nor any perceptual aspect of the object. In short, whereas categories of art disqualify certain sense modalities—internal structure, appearance under various conditions and from various distances, and so on—categories of nature do not.

If appropriate aesthetic appreciation is 'that appreciation of an object which reveals what aesthetic qualities and value it has' (Carlson 1984: 25), then in general there is no such thing as the appropriate aesthetic appreciation of nature. In the sense in which there is such a thing as *the* aesthetic qualities and value of a work of art, there is no such thing as *the* aesthetic qualities and value of nature. Of course, the truth-value of an aesthetic judgement about a natural item can be understood (as it usually is) as relative to a particular temporal slice of or stage in the item's natural history, a sensory mode, a level and manner of observation, and a perceptual aspect. But if not, the idea of the aesthetic value of a natural item is ill-defined. What are the aesthetic qualities and aesthetic value of a particular galaxy *qua* galaxy, a planet *qua* planet, a mountain *qua* mountain, a cloud *qua* cloud, a river *qua* river, a mango *qua* mango?[18] Perhaps the only viable conception of the aesthetic value of a natural item *qua* the natural item it is represents this value as being a function of the totality of positive and negative aesthetic qualities possessed by the item as an instance of its kind. If so, the multifaceted indefiniteness of this function underscores the problematic character of a positive aesthetics of nature.

[18] Is the appearance of a planet's star at sunrise and sunset an aspect of the aesthetic value of the planet *qua* planet—or perhaps of the star *qua* star? Are the reflections of trees on the bank an aspect of a river's aesthetic value *qua* river?

4

The Aesthetics of Nature: A Survey

> Nor ever yet
> The melting rainbow's vernal-tinctured hues
> To me have shone so pleasing, as when first
> The hand of science pointed out the path
> In which the sun-beams gleaming from the west
> Fall on the wat'ry cloud ...
>
> Mark Akenside, 'The Pleasures of Imagination'

4.1. INTRODUCTION

The long period of stagnation into which the aesthetics of nature fell after Hegel's relegation of natural beauty to a status inferior to the beauty of art was ended by Ronald Hepburn's ground-breaking (1966). In this essay, which offers a diagnosis of the causes of philosophy's neglect of the aesthetics of nature, Hepburn describes a number of kinds of aesthetic experience of nature that exhibit a variety of features that distinguish the aesthetic experience of nature from that of art and endow it with values different from those characteristic of the arts, thus making plain the harmful consequences of the neglect of natural beauty. The subtlety of Hepburn's thought precludes simple summary, and I will do no more than enumerate a few of his themes that have been taken up and developed in the now flourishing literature on the aesthetics of nature, although not always with the nuanced treatment accorded them by Hepburn. First, there is the idea that, through being both in and a part of nature, our aesthetic involvement with nature is typically both as actors and spectators. Second, there is the idea that, in contrast to what is typical of works of art, natural things are not set apart from their environment as objects of aesthetic interest—in other words, they are 'frameless'. Third, there is the idea that the aesthetic experience of nature should not be restricted to the contemplation of uninterpreted shapes, colours, patterns, and movements. Finally, there is the idea that the imaginative realization of the forces or processes that are responsible for a natural thing's appearance or that are active in a natural phenomenon is a principal activity in the aesthetic experience of nature.

4.2.   AN AESTHETICS OF ENGAGEMENT

Arnold Berleant (1993) stresses the first two of these ideas in the course of proposing what he calls an aesthetics of engagement for the aesthetic appreciation of nature (something he also recommends as a model for the appreciation of art), which represents the aesthetic subject as being an active participant in a condition of perceptual immersion in the natural world, with a sense of continuity of the subject's self with the forms and processes of nature, in place of traditional aesthetics, which is an aesthetics of disinterested contemplation, the subject being an observer distanced from a clearly circumscribed object of aesthetic interest. But, although the aesthetic appreciation of nature often requires the subject to be an active participant rather than a stationary spectator, an aesthetics of engagement is not a sound development from those two ideas and it suffers from three principal defects. First, as Hepburn (1998) has insisted, being essentially *in*, not over against, the landscape, does not prevent our aesthetic experience from being contemplative, which often it properly is. Second, the principal conception of the notion of disinterestedness in traditional aesthetics is Kant's, according to which a positive affective response to an item is disinterested only if it is not, or not just, pleasure in the satisfaction of a desire that the world should be a certain way. And disinterestedness of response in this sense is not only compatible with the various aspects of engagement that Berleant articulates that are aesthetic, but is a condition that, it seems, any satisfactory understanding of the notion of an aesthetic response must satisfy. Third, Berleant's rejection of both contemplation and disinterestedness, coupled with a failure to replace them with alternatives that are viable components of specifically aesthetic experience or appreciation, disqualifies his aesthetics of engagement with nature from being acceptable either as an account of nature appreciation or as a conception of aesthetic experience of nature.

4.3. ENVIRONMENTAL FORMALISM

One version of the view, rejected by Hepburn, that aesthetic appreciation consists in the aesthetic appreciation of uninterpreted things—things considered independently of the kinds they exemplify—is formalism. Environmental formalism is formalism about the aesthetic appreciation and evaluation of the natural environment. Allen Carlson (1979b) has developed an argument against environmental formalism built on the first two of Hepburn's ideas listed above. Formalism maintains that (i) aesthetic appreciation should be directed towards those aspects that constitute the form of an object, and (ii) the aesthetic value of an object is entirely determined by its formal qualities. The perceived form of an object consists of 'shapes, patterns, and designs'. Formal qualities are 'qualities of such forms, such as their being unified or chaotic, balanced or unbalanced, harmonious or confused'. So formal qualities are qualities that objects or combinations of objects have in virtue of their shapes, patterns, and designs. But these arise from or consist of the relations among the sensory qualities of objects—qualities of textures, colours, and lines. So in a wider sense the perceived form of an object consists of textures, colours, lines, shapes, patterns, and designs. It is this wider notion of perceived form that figures in Carlson's understanding of the doctrine of formalism. Accordingly, environmental formalism holds that in the aesthetic appreciation of the natural environment one must abstract from the nature of the items that compose the environment—land, water, vegetation, or hills, valleys, rivers, trees, and so on—and focus solely on the environment's perceived form, its lines, colours, and textures and the relations in which they stand to one another; and that a portion of nature is aesthetically appealing in so far as its perceived form is unified, balanced, possesses unity in variety, or whatever, and aesthetically unappealing in so far as it is disharmonious or lacks integration.

The essence of Carlson's argument against environmental formalism is this: A crucial difference between traditional art objects and the natural environment is that whereas works of art are 'framed or delimited in some formal way', the natural environment is not. And this entails a difference between the formal qualities of traditional works of art and those of the natural environment. For the formal qualities of a traditional work of art 'are in large part determined by the frame': they 'are (or are not) unified or balanced within their frames and in relation to their frames'. Hence a work's formal qualities, the recognition of which must underpin a correct evaluation of the work, 'are an important determinate aspect of the work itself' and so can be easily appreciated. But by contrast it is only a framed view of the natural environment, not the environment itself, that possesses formal qualities: any part of the environment can be seen from indefinitely many different positions and framed in indefinitely many different ways, and whatever formal qualities it is seen to possess will be relative to the frame and the position of the observer, appearing unified or balanced from one position as framed in a certain manner, chaotic or unbalanced from a different position or when framed differently.

Now the conclusion that the natural environment does not itself possess formal qualities, but only appears to possess formal qualities when framed from particular positions, does not seem to make much, if any, dent in the doctrine of environmental formalism. For the formalist can concede the relativity of formal qualities to frames and points of view and so the necessity of framing to aesthetic appreciation and yet still maintain that the aesthetic appreciation of the natural environment consists in the appreciation of formal qualities—the different formal qualities presented by the environment as variously framed from whatever points of view an observer chooses. Furthermore, nobody would attempt to appreciate aesthetically the (entire) natural environment, as such. Rather, one engages in aesthetic appreciation of some segment of it, perhaps a single item, such as a tree, a cloud, or an iceberg, or a small set of items, which items do have formal qualities, considered in themselves, independent of their location in the environment. And if no segmentation of the natural environment can be incorrect from the aesthetic point of view, an unframed appreciation of the formal qualities of a segment of the natural environment is not only possible but impervious to aesthetic criticism.

The conclusion Carlson favours is the stronger claim, that the natural environment as such does not possess formal qualities, by which he means that, *when appreciated aesthetically in the appropriate mode, it is not possible* to see it as having any formal qualities. His argument runs as follows: The appropriate mode of appreciation of the natural environment is 'the active, involved appreciation of one who is in the environment, being a part of and reacting to it'. But:

> In framing a section of the environment, one must become a static observer who is separate from that section and who views it from a specific external point. But one cannot be engaged in the appropriate active, involved appreciation while maintaining the static, external point of view required by framing. In short, one cannot both be in the environment which one appreciates and frame that environment; if one appreciates the environment by being in it, it is not a framed environment which one appreciates. (109–10)

But this argument is not compelling. It is true that when surrounded by the natural environment we can interact with it and must be active in it if we are not to miss aspects of it not perceivable from the position we happen to occupy at any particular time. But this does not mean that we must be constantly on the move to be deemed to be appreciating nature aesthetically in the appropriate mode. Even if the appropriate mode of aesthetic appreciation of the natural environment is of the active, involved kind, this should not be understood to imply that one must never become a static observer on pain of forfeiting one's right to be thought of as engaged in the aesthetic appreciation of the environment. There is nothing amiss in being a static observer of an ever changing sky-scape or a volcanic eruption, and choosing a spot to stop at and contemplate a scene from is a proper part of the aesthetic appreciation of the natural environment, not something inconsistent with it. So Carlson has not established that the natural environment cannot be appreciated and valued aesthetically in terms of its formal qualities because the appropriate mode of aesthetic appreciation precludes this.

Nevertheless, environmental formalism's insistence that the aesthetic appreciation of the natural environment must not be directed at items in the environment conceptualized as what they are (clouds, trees, valleys, and so on) is certainly unwarranted, being a product of a conception of aesthetic appreciation that without adequate justification restricts aesthetic experience to experience of items in abstraction from the kinds they exemplify, a conception little better suited to the aesthetic appreciation of the natural environment than to that of art.

4.4. NATURE'S EXPRESSIVE QUALITIES

The alternative Carlson proposes (1979*b*) to environmental formal-ism is that the natural environment must be appreciated and valued aesthetically in terms of its various non-formal aesthetic qualities, such as expressive qualities (serenity, majesty, and sombreness, for example) and qualities like gracefulness, delicacy, and garishness. Accordingly, 'in order to appreciate and value the aesthetic quality of the environment, we must appreciate and value qualities such as the gracefulness of an antelope, the delicacy of a flower, the austerity of a desert landscape, the serenity of a quiet meadow, or the omin-ousness of the sky before a storm' (Carlson 1977: 158). One weak-ness with this proposal is the uncertainty of the range and nature of expressive qualities. If austerity is severe simplicity, serenity tran-quillity (lack of disturbance), ominousness the property of being threatening, and majesty the property of being grand (imposing), then (i) a desert landscape is *literally* austere (severely simple), a quiet meadow serene (lacking in disturbances), the sky before a storm ominous (indicative of an approaching threat), and a mountain range majestic (imposing in virtue of being grand, and so inspiring fear, respect, or awe), and (ii) no specifically aesthetic sensibility is needed to detect the austerity, serenity, ominousness, and majesty, so that on one understanding of the aesthetic, they are not *aesthetic* qualities. But if this is typical of so-called expressive qualities, expressive qualities will be limited to those qualities that items liter-ally possess, a non-standard use of the notion and one that, it seems, Carlson himself does not embrace. For elsewhere Carlson elucidates the idea of expressive qualities by stating that the term 'expressive quality' refers to 'a fairly wide range of human values, emotions and attitudes which are associated with objects such that it is appropriate to say that an object *expresses* these values, emotions, and attitudes', cites the musical expression of sadness, melancholy, or joy as a case in point, and asserts that the 'relevant concept of "expression" is of the kind initially clarified by Santayana' (Carlson 1976: 75–6, 82 endnote 12). And this suggests either that the kind of understanding suggested above of austerity, serenity, ominousness, and majesty is mistaken—'majestic' could, of course, be understood to import the ideas of dignity and nobility, properties that a mountain range does not literally possess—or that Carlson's notion of expressive qualities accommodates qualities of heterogeneous kinds. It is regrettable that, although in recent years a considerable body of work has been done on expression in art, no satisfactory account has been given of the experience of nature as the bearer of expressive properties (despite the notable attempt of Wollheim (1991), criticized by Budd (2001a)).

But, however the notion of expressive qualities should best be understood, it follows from another observation of Carlson's that, given the aesthetic relevance to the appreciation of nature of the non-formal qualitites Carlson indicates, the aesthetic appreciation of nature cannot be restricted to qualities perceivable in items unconceptualized as or in abstraction from the kinds of things they are. For the perception of various non-formal qualities requires a certain amount of knowledge of the nature of the environment or the portion of nature being appreciated:

one who has only perceptual sensibility may be able to see the balance of a mountain landscape, without much knowledge of the environment in question. But to feel the determination and the tenacity expressed by the trees which grow on the mountain slopes requires, in addition to sensibility, a knowledge and understanding of such trees and of the conditions under which they cling to life. Perceiving the majesty and power of the mountain range itself is certainly enhanced, if not made possible, by knowledge of how long it has existed and of the forces which brought it into being. Likewise, certain meadows and forest glens strike us as warm and serene once we know they are relatively secure homes and feeding grounds for the creatures who inhabit them. But if we knew, rather, that these same openings were avoided by such creatures for fear of predators, they would express quite different qualities—perhaps tension or ominousness. (Carlson 1977: 152)

Furthermore, the uncertain character of expressive qualities does not itself weaken the force of two arguments that Carlson has developed in which expressive qualities figure, one being directed specifically against environmental formalism, the other not. The argument directed specifically against environmental formalism (Carlson 1977) maintains that formalism cannot explain the loss of aesthetic value to the natural environment caused by various intrusions by humanity, such as the construction of a power line that passes through it. For from a formalist point of view a power line might not only be aesthetically attractive in itself but, taken together with its environment, constitute an aesthetically attractive formal design, even, perhaps, helping to frame or balance a view of the landscape. So what does explain the loss of aesthetic value? Carlson's answer is 'the non-formal aesthetic qualities of the natural environment which are affected by the actual presence of the power line and/or by its own non-formal aesthetic qualities':

For example, the relevant natural environment may have certain expressive qualities due to its apparent or actual remoteness, but the expression of these qualities may be inhibited by the presence of the power line, or the power line may itself have certain expressive qualities which, unlike its formal qualities, do not 'fit' with the expressive qualities of the natural environment. (159)

The idea, then, is that the expressive qualities of the power line, perhaps aggression and power, might be incongruous with the expressive qualities of the natural environment, perhaps tranquillity.

Carlson's other argument (1976) is a defence of the view—the 'eyesore argument'—that one good reason why the natural environment should be cleaned of the human detritus that clutters it is because (i) such refuse is not aesthetically pleasing, and (ii) an aesthetically pleasing environment is preferable to one that is not. The line of attack on the argument that Carlson is concerned to counter exploits a particular form of aestheticism, *camp sensibility*, defined by Susan Sontag (1964) as 'the consistently aesthetic experience of the world', which can transform one's experience such that what was aesthetically unpleasing or displeasing becomes aesthetically pleasing—as with 'turn-of-the-century picture postcards', 'old Flash Gordon comics', 'feather boas', and 'Aubrey Beardsley drawings' (Sontag's examples). Objects that might be thought of as lacking in aesthetic appeal, or being in bad taste, if attended to in a new way—one that emphasizes 'texture, sensuous surface, and style at the expense of content' (Sontag) or seeks for the objects' symbolic or expressive qualities—can become a source of aesthetic gratification, so that 'The kewpie doll, the Christmas card, the Tiffany lampshade can be enjoyed aesthetically, not for their beauty but for the bizarre qualities and their implicit reflection of social attitudes' (Beardsley 1970). The objection that Carlson wishes to counter is that there is a cheap alternative to removing the refuse: if the refuse is initially found aesthetically displeasing, just develop one's camp sensibility so that the refuse becomes aesthetically pleasing. He meets this objection in two ways. The first concedes that the camp alternative to cleaning up the environment works fine against the eyesore argument in the sense in which something can be aesthetically pleasing in virtue of its colours, shapes, textures, patterns (the 'thin sense'), but not in the sense in which something can be aesthetically pleasing in virtue of these *and* its expressive qualities (the 'thick sense').[1] For (i) the expressive qualities of litter are such qualities as waste, disregard, and carelessness, and (ii) although camp sensibility can make us more aware of such qualities, most of us are unable to enjoy aesthetically the expression of such qualities. Furthermore, if we are unable to find an object aesthetically pleasing in the thick sense because of the negative nature of its expressive qualities, this often makes it difficult or impossible to aesthetically enjoy the object in the thin sense. Hence, if camp sensibility makes us more aware of an item's negative expressive qualities, it will render us unable to enjoy it aesthetically at all. Accordingly, an object with such negative expressive qualities cannot be aesthetically enjoyed by adopting camp sensibility. But since this argument depends on two empirical claims that might be contested, Carlson offers the following sketch of an alternative line of argument—a moral-aesthetic argument. To enjoy aesthetically the expressive qualities of refuse would be to condone the values and attitudes that are responsible for it and in virtue of which it possesses those expressive qualities, since aesthetic enjoyment of something counts against wishing to eliminate it. But these values and attitudes—waste, disregard, carelessness—are morally unacceptable, and condoning the morally unacceptable is itself morally unacceptable. Accordingly, even if it is possible to enjoy litter aesthetically (in the thick sense), morally we should not.

Carlson's (1977), and to some extent his (1976), has been critically examined by Yuriko Saito (1984). But her focus shifts away from aesthetically unfortunate intrusions of humanity into nature to the destruction of nature. And the dilemma she ends by facing Carlson with—if a purely aesthetic standpoint is adopted, abusive treatment of nature does not always spoil nature's aesthetic value, but if aesthetic judgement is affected by ethical considerations, it is for ethical, not aesthetic, reasons, that abusive treatment is undesirable—is ineffective against a position, one embraced by Carlson (1986), that does not conceive of the aesthetic as a realm impermeable by ethical considerations.

---

[1] Carlson considers roadside clutter to be unsightly primarily because of its [negative] expressive qualities.

4.5. THE AESTHETIC APPRECIATION OF NATURE AS NATURE

Given that the aesthetic appreciation of nature should not be thought of as the aesthetic appreciation of arrays of uninterpreted particulars, how should it be understood? A surprisingly popular conception, one that aligns the aesthetic appreciation of nature extremely closely with the appreciation of art, represents the aesthetic appreciation of nature as consisting in nature's being regarded as if it were art. This conception is often built into claims about the essence of aesthetic interest or the nature of the aesthetic attitude. For example, Stephen Davies asserts that 'an aesthetic interest is an interest in something for the sake of the pleasure that comes from regarding it as a work of art (if it is one) or as if it were a work of art (if it is not)' (Davies 1991: 49). And Richard Wollheim (1980, §§40–2), who construes the aesthetic attitude as the attitude of regarding something as a work of art, maintains that 'cases where what we regard as a work of art is, in point of fact, a piece of uncontrived nature' are peripheral or second-ary cases of the aesthetic attitude (the central cases being those where what is regarded as a work of art has been produced as a work of art). Accordingly, to adopt the aesthetic attitude towards some portion of nature is to regard that portion of nature as if it were a work of art.[2]

Now it is undoubtedly true, as has often been observed, that the aesthetic appreciation of the natural world has, at certain times, been influenced by the representation of nature in art, leading people to appreciate hitherto neglected aspects of nature or to see nature as nature had been represented in art (as with the eighteenth-century use of 'Claude glasses')—although this influence seems to have been restricted more or less to landscape, rather than individual flora and fauna, say, and those influenced were the appreciators of certain styles of pictorial art, not the artists responsible for that art. But even if this influence had been much more widespread, it would not licence an *identification* of the aesthetic appreciation of nature with the appreciation of nature as if it were art.[3] Moreover, it is clear that

[2] This view of the essence of aesthetic interest or the nature of the aesthetic attitude, which presupposes the logical priority of the concept of art over that of the aesthetic, is vulnerable to the argument that Frank Sibley brings against it in (Sibley 2001*b*).

[3] Stephen Davies (1994: 246 n. 56) has claimed that 'we appreciate natural sounds aesthetically only by approaching them as if they were musical, which is to hear them via the musical conventions in which we are versed. People from different musical

any version of the view that the aesthetic appreciation of nature consists in regarding nature as if it were art will be defective. First, the claim that this is in fact how we *do* appreciate nature when we appreciate nature aesthetically is vulnerable to the charge that it is untrue to the phenomenology of the aesthetic experience of nature— at least, to the character of my own and many others' experience. For me, the aesthetic appreciation of nature is impregnated with an unclouded awareness that nature is not of humanity's making but a product of natural forces and processes, and that what confronts me includes an astonishing profusion of forms and ways of life remarkably different from our own. Second, there could not be a successful argument that takes us from the undeniable fact that it is possible to regard a natural object as if it were a work of art to the conclusion that this is how we must or should regard natural objects when we experience them aesthetically.[4] Furthermore, the claim that this is how we *must* appreciate nature in order to appreciate nature aesthetically since there is no alternative is manifestly false. And the claim that this is how we *should* appreciate nature aesthetically if we are to derive the greatest aesthetic satisfaction from or find the greatest aesthetic value in nature stands unsupported without some kind of measure that decides in favour of this attitude to nature rather than any alternatives.

The rejection of this conception of the aesthetic appreciation of nature raises the question of what the correct alternative is. The obvious alternative is that the aesthetic appreciation of nature should be thought of as the aesthetic appreciation of nature *as* nature—more particularly, the aesthetic appreciation of a natural item *as the natural item it is*.[5] (Compare artistic appreciation, which is the appreciation of art *as* art, so that, accordingly, the artistic appreciation of a particular work of art is the appreciation of it *as the work of art it is*, which involves experiencing it under the concept of the kind of work it is, as a painting rather than a colour photograph, for example.) This conception of the aesthetic appreciation of nature does not imply that

cultures hear natural sounds differently. Just as there can be no musically naive response to musical works qua music, there can be no naive aesthetic response to natural sounds.' But the claim is too strong. Even in the case of birdsong, which is what Davies has principally in mind, our musical experience does not need to mould our perception on pain of our failing to respond aesthetically to the sounds.

[4] See Essay 3, §2.
[5] See Essay 1.

aesthetic judgements about works of art—judgements about the aesthetic properties of works of art—aspire to and are capable of being objectively true, aesthetic judgements about nature are condemned to relativity. In other words, the view he opposes is that whereas a work of art really does possess certain aesthetic properties, so that it is straightforwardly true that it is exuberant, serene, or full of a sense of mystery, for example, natural items can properly be thought of as possessing certain aesthetic properties only relative to whatever the way may be in which someone happens to perceive that item. His argument turns on ideas developed by Kendall Walton.

Walton (1970) has shown, with respect to works of art, that (i) what aesthetic properties an item *appears* to possess—what aesthetic properties we perceive or experience the item as possessing—is a function of the category or categories under which it is experienced (i.e. what sort of thing it is perceived as being), and (ii) what aesthetic properties an item *really* possesses is determined by the right categories to experience the item as falling under—it really possesses those aesthetic properties it appears to possess when perceived (by a duly sensitive person, under the appropriate conditions, and so on) in the *right* or *correct* categories to experience the item as belonging to. The aesthetic significance of the categories under which a work is perceived is due to the fact that various non-aesthetic perceptual features are what Walton calls 'standard', 'variable', or 'contra-standard' with respect to a ('perceptually distinguishable') category, and the perceived aesthetic character of a work is a function of which of its non-aesthetic perceptual features are standard, variable, or contra-standard for one who perceives the work under that category. Walton's best-known illustration of his claim that what aesthetic properties a work seems to possess is (partly) dependent on which of its features are standard, which variable, and which contra-standard for the perceiver (and so dependent on which categories the person experiences the work under) is of an imaginary society that does not have an established medium of painting, but does produce a kind of work of art called 'guernicas', a 'guernica' being like a version of Picasso's painting *Guernica* done in bas-relief; that is, it is a surface with the colours and shapes of Picasso's painting but moulded to protrude from the wall like a relief map of some terrain, 'guernicas' being distinguished from one another by the different geometrical natures of their surfaces. Picasso's *Guernica*, when seen as a painting, is seen as dynamic, violent, disturbing, but when seen as a 'guernica' would be seen differently—as cold and lifeless, or serene and restful, or bland, dull, boring, or whatever.

The question is whether Walton's two theses transfer to nature, as Carlson argues they do. The essence of Carlson's argument is this: The psychological thesis, (i), does so transfer. That is, it is at least sometimes true that what aesthetic properties a natural item appears to possess is a function of the category under which it is experienced. For consider, first, the aesthetic appreciation of a natural object—an animal of a certain species, say. If we have some knowledge of what is standard for animals of that species—their adult size, for example—this knowledge will affect the aesthetic properties an animal of that kind, perceived as such, appears to us to possess, if, for example, it falls far short of, or is considerably greater than, that standard size. Thus Shetland ponies are perceived as charming, cute, and Clydesdale horses are perceived as majestic, lumbering, when perceived as belonging to, and judged with respect to, the category of horses. Consider, second, the aesthetic appreciation of the natural environment. Here is an example of Hepburn's:

Suppose I am walking over a wide expanse of sand and mud. The quality of the scene is perhaps that of wild, glad emptiness. But suppose I bring to bear upon the scene my knowledge that this is a tidal basin, the tide being out. The realization is not aesthetically irrelevant. I see myself now as walking on what is for half the day sea-bed. The wild glad emptiness may be tempered by a disturbing weirdness. (Hepburn 1966: 295)

(Note, though, that the aesthetic properties a natural item is experienced as possessing might well *not* change if the item is experienced first under one natural category—say a category it does not in fact belong to—and then under another—one it does belong to: the apparent aesthetic properties of a heavenly body that I have landed on, considering it to be a planet, need not be vulnerable to the later realization that it is not a planet, but a moon.)

What about the philosophical thesis, (ii)? Are there, from the aesthetic point of view, correct and incorrect categories in which nature can be perceived, or should the correctness or otherwise of aesthetic judgements about nature, unlike those about art, be understood as relative to whatever category someone happens to perceive something natural as falling under? If there are such categories, then the 'category-relative interpretation' of aesthetic judgements about nature—the interpretation of them as implicitly containing a reference to some particular category or set of categories, so that apparently opposed judgements about the aesthetic properties of a natural item are compatible—is mistaken. Carlson's answer is that there are correct categories, both for natural objects and the natural environment. These are the categories, established by natural history and natural science, that the natural item falls under: the correct categories are the categories of nature that natural items actually belong to.

The main difficulty that needs to be overcome if the philosophical thesis is to be transferred successfully to nature is the establishment of the correct categories (if there are such) in which nature can be perceived, which means *which* of those concepts of nature a natural item falls under—for it falls under many—it should be perceived under *from the aesthetic point of view*, where this means that perception under those concepts discloses the aesthetic properties it really possesses and thereby makes possible a proper assessment of its aesthetic value. A crucial fact is that, unlike art, which of the categories a natural item belongs to are the correct categories to aesthetically appreciate it under is not determined by the idea of appreciating it *as nature*. For example, the reason, in the case of art, for prioritizing a more specific category to which an item belongs over a less specific category to which it belongs—for identifying the more specific category as *the* correct category to perceive the item under from the aesthetic point of view—where the artist intended it to be perceived not just under the more general category but under the more specific category, is lacking in the case of nature. On the other hand, a reason would need to be provided for prioritizing a less specific category— for insisting that a Shetland pony or a Clydesdale should be perceived not under the category *Shetland pony* or *Clydesdale*, but under the category *horse*. In the absence of such reasons, neither a more specific nor a more general category can be deemed the correct category, in which case a natural item cannot be deemed to possess a particular set of aesthetic properties, but will possess contrasting sets for at least some of the categories of which it is a member. But, in any case, there are important disanalogies between art and nature which render the application of the philosophical thesis to nature problematic, and which are relevant to an assessment of the doctrine of positive aesthetics with respect to nature, a view embraced by many who have been entranced by the variety and profusion, the apparently omnipresent beauty, of the natural world.

4.7. POSITIVE AESTHETICS[8]

Positive aesthetics with respect to nature maintains that from the aesthetic point of view nature is unlike art in that negative aesthetic evaluative judgements are out of place—out of place because *pristine* nature is essentially aesthetically good; that is, always has a positive aesthetic value.[9] Two linked questions immediately arise: What exactly is the force of this doctrine? and: Is there any good reason to embrace it? Clearly, the acceptability of the doctrine depends on what form it takes, and it can assume many different forms in accordance with the answers it gives to three kinds of question: (i) of scope (what elements or aspects or divisions of nature it applies to), (ii) of strength (whether, for example, it disallows the attribution of negative aesthetic qualities to nature, or disallows comparative judgements about natural items that assign a higher aesthetic value to one item than to another), and (iii) of modal status (Godlovitch 1998*a,b*).

It would be a very small step from the proposition that no natural item, or combination of items, untouched by humanity possesses negative aesthetic qualities to the conclusion that every natural item, or array of such items, unaffected by humanity has a positive overall aesthetic value—a step vanishingly small given the kind of freedom that characterizes the aesthetic appreciation of nature.[10] For this freedom guarantees that any natural item will offer something of positive aesthetic value, something that is aesthetically rewarding, even if the rewards are very small. But while it is clear that nature is immune to many of the defects to which works of art are liable—nature cannot be trite, sentimental, badly drawn, crude, insipid, derivative, mere pastiche, for example—the premise is questionable, holding true for, at most, items that are not, or do not contain, forms of life. A negative aesthetic quality is a quality that, considered in itself, makes a negative contribution to an item's aesthetic value and

---

[8] For a fuller treatment of the doctrine of positive aesthetics see Essay 3, §4.

[9] As noted in Essay 3 n. 5, pristine nature, understood as nature unaffected by humanity, now includes relatively little, perhaps nothing at all, within the biosphere. But in some cases the effects of humanity are minimal, and the effects of humanity can disappear entirely, as when a piece of land reverts to its former, perhaps natural, state, displaying the same diversity and proportion of flora as in the surrounding area, so that a portion of nature once affected by humanity might at a later date properly be thought of as pristine again.

[10] See §8.

so constitutes an aesthetic defect in the item. For a work of art to possess a negative aesthetic quality in the relevant sense, it must be defective as a work of art. Likewise, for a natural item to possess a negative aesthetic quality it must be defective as a product of nature. But this means that it must be defective as an instance of the kind of natural thing it is. And this is possible only for forms of life: a cloud, a sea, a boulder, cannot be a defective cloud, sea, or boulder, for the kinds of things they are—clouds, seas, boulders—lack natural functions that particular instances of them might not be well suited to perform. But a member of a species can be a defective instance of that species, malformed, unable to function in one or more ways normal for the species, perhaps disabling it from flourishing in the manner characteristic of the species, and only living things can be in an unhealthy state, be ill, decline, and die. Hence, an adherent of the view that a natural thing cannot possess a negative aesthetic quality would need to show that none of the ways in which organisms can be defective instances of their kinds could be manifest in their appearance in such a manner as to display a negative aesthetic quality. It does not seem possible to establish this.

If the possibility that nothing in virgin nature, or nothing within the scope of the doctrine of positive aesthetics, can possess negative aesthetic qualities, qualities that, unless outweighed, would endow their subject with a negative aesthetic value overall, is left aside, arguments for a positive aesthetics of nature—arguments that do not rest on that assumption—do not appear compelling. Allen Carlson (1984) has demolished three arguments that might be offered in support of the doctrine, but has provided two of his own, one (1984) based on the claim that positive aesthetic considerations partly determine the categories that are created by science to render the natural world intelligible, the other (1993) maintaining that the appreciation of nature must be understood as a form of so-called 'order appreciation', which implies that the appreciation of nature consists in the selection of objects of appreciation in the natural world and focuses on the order (the natural order) imposed on them by the forces of nature, the selection, 'which makes the natural order visible and intelligible', being governed by the story given by natural science.

It is unclear exactly which version of positive aesthetics with respect to nature these arguments are intended to establish. But it is clear that they certainly fail to establish the most ambitious version of positive aesthetics—that *each individual* natural item, *at each moment of its existence* (or, slightly weaker, *considered throughout its duration*) has a roughly equal positive overall aesthetic value; and there are reasons for believing that it is not possible to show that the most ambitious version of positive aesthetics is correct.[11] To change the scope of the doctrine of positive aesthetics from *individuals* to *kinds* would effect no alteration in the doctrine unless sense can be given to the idea of a kind possessing a positive aesthetic value which does not reduce to the idea that each instance of the kind has that value. But even if this is possible—perhaps it would be possible to invoke the idea of a normal instance of the kind—the doctrine would still be hazardous. One reason is the diversity of categories of nature, introducing different principles of identity and individuation for the items that belong to them and covering such different phenomena as mere visual appearances, items defined as what they are by the use made of them, and ones defined by what has brought them about or by their relation to other natural items. Think, for instance, of the categories of cloud, tributary, seashell, gust of wind, stamen, sky, forest, egg, flash-flood, geyser, cave, stalactite, lodge or nest, eye of storm, swamp, herd, school, or swarm, bone, snakeskin, dune or wave, nut, eclipse, fossil, aurora. Given this diversity, given that pristine nature was *not* flawlessly designed for aesthetic contemplation or appreciation by human beings, and on the assumption that natural things *are* possible subjects of negative aesthetic qualities, it would be remarkable if everything in nature, no matter how nature is cut at the joints, were to have a roughly equal positive overall aesthetic value.

4.8. FREEDOM, RELATIVITY, OBJECTIVITY, AND POSITIVE AESTHETICS[12]

I can now make good my claim (§6) about the existence and significance of disanalogies between art and nature with respect to the constraints imposed on appropriate appreciation by the relevant categories to which the items belong, and indicate the consequences this has for the idea of a natural item's aesthetic properties and value

---

[11] See Essay 3, §4.   [12] Compare Essay 3, §5.

and so for the viability of the transference to nature of Walton's philosophical thesis and for the plausibility of the doctrine of positive aesthetics with respect to nature.

The various art forms are sometimes divided into those for which the members are abstract types (such as composed music) and those for which the members are spatio-temporal individuals (such as paintings). But some philosophers reject the distinction, maintaining that all works of art are types. Whichever position is to be preferred, individual natural items differ from works of art in ways that have far-reaching consequences for the aesthetic properties they can properly be deemed to possess considered as the things they are and for their overall aesthetic value as natural things. First, lacking the immutability of abstract types, they are subject to change and the changes they undergo will result in the possession of different aesthetic properties at different times; and, unlike what is characteristic of works of art that are mutable spatio-temporal individuals (if any are), they lack both an optimal condition, according to their creator's intention, in which their aesthetic properties are manifest and a dilapidated condition in which their true aesthetic properties are no longer displayed. Second, the relation between the category of art that a work belongs to and the appropriate artistic appreciation of that work is very different from the relation between the category of nature that an item belongs to and the appropriate aesthetic appreciation of that item as the natural item it is. For whereas a work's artistic category (i) is definitive of the mode of perception required for the appreciation of the work, if there is a single mode, or of the various modes, if more than one is necessary, or of the order in which the work's contents should be assimilated, if no particular mode or set of modes is necessary, (ii) renders certain modes of perception and engagement with the work inappropriate, and (iii) indicates how the appropriate mode (or modes) of perception should be employed—at what it should (or should not) be directed and under what conditions—a natural thing's natural category does none of these things. Accordingly, not only do a natural item's aesthetic properties change over time as it undergoes change, without any set constituting *the* aesthetic properties of the item *qua* the natural item it is, but its appearance is affected by climatic conditions, the observer's point of view, season, time of day, sense modality employed, power of magnification or amplification, and so on, none of these being optimal or mandatory, so that the range of its aesthetic properties or aesthetically relevant appearances is typically open-ended in a manner uncharacteristic of works of art. The lack of constraints imposed by categories of nature on the aesthetic appreciation of items in its domain endows the aesthetic appreciation of nature with a distinctive kind of freedom.

Now either the truth-value of a judgement about the aesthetic properties and value of a natural item is understood, as usually it is, in a relative manner—as relative to a particular stage in the item's natural history, a perceptual mode, a level and manner of observation, and a perceptual aspect—or it is not. If it is not, then in general there is no such thing as the appropriate aesthetic appreciation of nature, if by this is meant 'that appreciation of an object which reveals what aesthetic qualities and value it has' (Carlson 1984), and the idea of a natural item's aesthetic value, considered as the natural thing it is, is ill-defined, often being plagued in particular by irresoluble uncertainty as to the relevance or irrelevance to its own aesthetic value of one or another aspect of the world in which the thing is involved.[13] (To employ a conception of the aesthetic value of a natural item *qua* the natural item it is as the sum of its positive and negative aesthetic qualities considered as an instance of its kind would be to use a notion that is multiply indefinite and renders the aesthetic value of everything in nature uncertain, as is especially obvious in the case of such natural items as mountains, rivers, or storms, for example.) Accordingly, through its uncritical use of the notion of a natural item's aesthetic value, the doctrine of a positive aesthetics of nature, advanced in a version that does not disallow the possession of negative aesthetic qualities by natural items, and understood as a thesis about instances of kinds of natural thing, must have an uncertain status.

4.9. MODELS OF NATURE APPRECIATION

Carlson has suggested that we need a model of the aesthetic appreciation of nature, and in particular of the natural environment, that will indicate *what* is to be aesthetically appreciated and *how* it is to be

---

[13] The artistic value of works of art that diverge from what is or has been characteristic of art is, to the extent that there is such a divergence, subject to the indefiniteness that characterizes the aesthetic value of nature.

aesthetically appreciated—something we have a good grasp of in the case of works of art. In the case of art we generally know what to appreciate in that we can distinguish a work and its parts from anything else and its aesthetically relevant aspects from those that are not aesthetically relevant; and we generally know how to appreciate in that we know what actions to perform in order to appreciate the work. But what about the natural environment? This is problematic because of a vital difference between art and nature. Our knowledge of what and how to appreciate in the case of art stems from the fact that works of art are our own creations and the products of intentional actions. But nature is not our creation.

At least five models are present in the literature: (i) the object model, (ii) the landscape (or scenery) model, (iii) the natural-environment model, (iv) the arousal model, and (v) the aloofness (or mystery) model.

(i) The *object model* maintains that the aesthetic appreciation of nature consists in the appreciation of a natural object as the actual physical object it is and the qualities to be aesthetically appreciated are limited to the sensuous and design qualities of the actual object (colour, shape, texture, pattern) and its abstract expressive qualities (if it has any). On this model, to engage in aesthetic appreciation of nature a natural object must be removed, actually or contemplatively, from its surroundings and attention focused on its sensuous, design, and expressive qualities. Accordingly, a piece of rock, removed or contemplated in abstraction from its surroundings, might be appreciated for its wonderfully smooth and gracefully curved surface and for its being expressive of solidity.

In arguing against the object model as an appropriate model for the aesthetic appreciation of nature, Carlson (1979a) draws a distinction between appreciating nature and appreciating the objects of nature. While it is certainly possible to aesthetically appreciate an object of nature in the way indicated by the object model, the object model is an inadequate model for the aesthetic appreciation of nature. For, in virtue of the required (actual or contemplative) removal of a natural object from its surroundings, it imposes a severe limitation on the aesthetic appreciation of natural objects, and may involve a falsification of their aesthetic qualities. In the case of art objects that are 'self-contained aesthetic units':

neither the environment of their creation nor the environment of display are [*sic*] aesthetically relevant: the removal of a self-contained art object from its environment of creation will not vary its aesthetic qualities and the environment of display should not affect its aesthetic qualities. However, natural objects possess what we might call an organic unity with their environment of creation: such objects are a part of and have developed out of the elements of their environments by means of the forces at work within those environments. Thus the environments of creation are aesthetically relevant to natural objects. And for this reason the environments of display are equally relevant in virtue of the fact that these environments will be either the same as or different from the environments of creation. In either case the aesthetic qualities of natural objects will be affected. (130)

So in its environment of creation the piece of rock will not be just wonderfully smooth, gracefully curved, and expressive of solidity. In fact, it may well lack the final quality. For qualities that are the product of the relationship between the object and its environment accrue to the object when in (and considered in) its environment of creation:

It is here expressive of the particular forces which shaped and continue to shape it and displays for aesthetic appreciation its place in and its relation to its environment. (130)

And, depending upon its place in that environment, it may not express solidity.

In sum: On the one hand, if a natural object is removed (in reality or thought) from its environment, the object model provides an account of what and how to appreciate the object, but narrows the aesthetic qualities open to appreciation to a relatively small set. On the other hand, if the natural object is to be appreciated in and in relation to its environment, it is an inadequate model for a very large part of the relevant appreciation, and so fails to provide an adequate account of what to appreciate in nature and how to appreciate it.

Now the object model, considered as *the* model for the aesthetic appreciation of nature, is certainly inadequate, for the aesthetic appreciation of nature encompasses much more than the appreciation of natural objects capable of being removed from their environments of creation—as with Kant's favourite example of the sublime, the star-studded night sky, or with rivers, mountains, forests, deserts, and so on. Furthermore, unless the idea of environment of creation is understood in an excessively wide sense, many natural things (sentient creatures) leave their environment of creation for another environment or migrate from one to another. Moreover, if the environment of creation of a bird, say, is the nest in which it was hatched, that environment seems to have nothing to do with the aesthetic appreciation of a bird as a natural thing. But, leaving all that aside, how effective is Carlson's argument in the case of detachable natural objects?

It suffers from two weaknesses. In the first place, it is not necessary for an object actually to be in its environment of creation for it to be appreciated for qualities that are a product of the relationship between the object and its environment: to appreciate the wonderful smoothness of a rock as an effect of erosion by the sea—not the environment of creation of *the rock*, but the environment of creation of *its wonderful smoothness*, which is the product of the forces at work in the sea—it is not necessary for it still to be in the sea or washed up on the shore. So it does not follow from the supposed relevance of a natural object's environment of creation to its aesthetic appreciation that its environment of display is also relevant to its aesthetic appreciation (as nature). Second, Carlson's argument turns on (i) a natural object's position in its environment of creation, and (ii) the object's having developed out of the elements of its environment by means of the forces at work in that environment. The first factor appears to figure in Carlson's argument only in combination with the second: what qualities (solidity, for example) it 'appears' to be expressive of when considered in itself may not be qualities it is expressive of in its environment of creation—whether that is so will depend on its place in that environment. If it is intended to play an additional role, drawing attention to the aesthetic relevance of the relations in which it stands to other items in its environment, it lacks force. The qualities available to its aesthetic appreciation (as a natural object) that it possesses in virtue of its intrinsic nature are not disqualified from being the focus of aesthetic appreciation (of nature) just because if it were to be considered in the relations in which it stands to other parts of its environment, these qualities would not be salient and other features (its harmonious relation with another element of the environment, or a pattern of which it composes a part), absent from the aesthetic appreciation of the object considered in itself, would become prominent. But, in any case, Carlson's example of a change of apparent expressive quality brought about by perceiving a natural object not in abstraction from but in relation to its environment of creation is unconvincing. Solidity does not imply invulnerability to natural forces. Accordingly, even if in its natural setting it is manifest that the rock's smoothness and shape is the result of natural forces and that its smoothness, shape, and unity is subject to change by the continued operation of those or other natural forces, that provides no justification for the claim that its position in its environment of creation might determine that it is not expressive of solidity, a quality it appears to have when considered in isolation.

(ii) The *landscape model* maintains that the aesthetic appreciation of nature consists in appreciating nature as if it were a landscape painting, where 'landscape' means 'a prospect—usually a grandiose prospect—seen from a specific standpoint and distance' (Carlson 1979*a*).[14] So the model 'requires dividing the environment into scenes or blocks of scenery, each of which is to be viewed from a particular point by a viewer who is separated by the appropriate spatial (and emotional?) distance' (132). And the model centres 'attention on those aesthetic qualities of color and design which are seen and seen at a distance' (131).

Carlson's critique of this model is simple: the model is inappropriate to the actual nature of the object of appreciation, because it requires 'the appreciation of the environment not as what it is and with the qualities it has, but rather as something which it is not and with qualities it does not have'. For 'the environment is not a scene, not a representation, not static, and not two dimensional', whereas the model requires the environment to be viewed as if it were 'a static representation which is essentially "two dimensional" ', reducing the environment 'to a scene or view'.

Now Carlson slips between two understandings of the landscape model, the first presenting the appreciation of nature as the appreciation of nature as if it were a landscape painting, the second as a [grandiose] prospect seen from a specific vantage point (i.e. as what a landscape painting is a representation of):

the landscape model of appreciation . . . encourages perceiving and appreciating nature as if it were a landscape painting, as a grandiose prospect seen from a specific standpoint and distance (131)

---

[14] Grandiosity of prospect is obviously inessential to the landscape model, whatever role it has played in the history of the aesthetic appreciation of nature.

On the first understanding, the model is vulnerable to the objection that it is inappropriate to the actual nature of the object of appreciation: nature is not a representation (either two- or three-dimensional) of nature.[15] But on the second understanding it is not, since it does not require 'the appreciation of the environment not as what it is and with the qualities it has, but rather as something which it is not and with qualities it does not have'. The correct criticism of the landscape model, on the second understanding, is that it wrongly presents what is *an* appropriate mode of aesthetic appreciation of nature as being *the only* appropriate mode. Although the natural environment does afford prospects, it offers much more than this to aesthetic appreciation: the aesthetic appreciation of nature is not restricted to vision; and where appreciation does take place primarily through the eyes, the observer need not be stationary nor positioned at a point of view from which the landscape can be seen to unfold nor at a fair distance from what is being attended to nor focused on qualities of colour and overall design.

(iii) Carlson's proposed solution to the problem of the appropriate model is his *natural-environment model* (1979*a*). The leading idea of the natural-environment model is that to aesthetically appreciate nature for what it is and for the qualities it has, the fact that the natural environment is (a) natural, and (b) an environment must play a central role in the aesthetic appreciation of nature. Now an environment is our surroundings, the setting within which we exist, which we normally experience through all our senses, although usually only as background. To appreciate it aesthetically we must, using all our senses, foreground it—that, in outline, is how to aesthetically appreciate an environment. But the natural environment is natural, not a work of art, and as such has no boundaries or foci of aesthetic significance. So what is to be aesthetically appreciated in the natural environment? The answer is that the considerable common sense/scientific knowledge of nature that we possess, which

---

[15] The fact that nature is not static is not in itself a conclusive objection to the model, for, even without modifying the model to that of a motion picture of a landscape from a fixed vantage point, the different appearances nature presents as events unfold within it could be accommodated by construing the aesthetic appreciation of each different scene as the appreciation of a somewhat different landscape painting. But only a motion picture can provide a surrogate of movement in the natural world, so that to accommodate the appreciation of movement it would be necessary to replace the model of a landscape painting by that of a motion picture.

transforms our experience from what would otherwise be meaning-
less, indeterminate, and confused to meaningful, determinate, and
orderly, provides 'the appropriate foci of aesthetic significance and
the boundaries of the setting'. Accordingly, 'to aesthetically appreciate nature we must have knowledge of the different environments
of nature and of the systems and elements within those environments'. And, because there are different natural environments, how
to aesthetically appreciate the natural environment varies from environment to environment:

we must survey a prairie environment, looking at the subtle contours of the
land, feeling the wind blowing across the open space, and smelling the mix of
prairie grasses and flowers. But . . . in a dense forest environment . . . we must
examine and scrutinize, inspecting the detail of the forest floor, listening
carefully for the sounds of birds and smelling carefully for the scent of
spruce and pine. (273–4)

In appropriately appreciating . . . a natural environment such as an alpine
meadow it is useful to know, for instance, that it has developed under
constraints imposed by the climate of high altitude, and that diminutive
size in flora is an adaptation to such constraints. This knowledge can guide
our framing of the environment so that, for example, we avoid imposing
inappropriately large frames, which may cause us to simply overlook mini-
ature wild flowers. In such a case we will neither appreciatively note their
wonderful adjustment to their situation nor even attune our senses to their
subtle fragrance, texture and hue. (Carlson 1992: 141–2)

Furthermore, a requirement of the natural environment model—one
that Carlson uses against the object model—is that the appreciation
of a natural item, whether or not it is still in its environment of
creation, must, on pain of misrepresenting the item's expressive
properties, involve the consideration of it as located in its environment of creation and shaped by the forces at work in that environment.

There are many problems with the natural-environment model. I
will highlight two problems of scope that afflict it. First, there is the
question of the intended scope of the model. Although focused on
the appreciation of the natural environment, it appears to be offered
as the correct model not just for appreciation of the natural environment, but for aesthetic appreciation of nature *tout court*. But this
would be to identify the aesthetic appreciation of nature (as nature)
with the aesthetic appreciation of the natural environment, and

would rule out the possibility of aesthetically appreciating a natural object which is not in its natural environment of creation, unless in appreciating it it is considered in imagination in relation to its place and history in its former context. But trees planted in towns, for example, can be aesthetically appreciated as being natural objects, even though they are located in and have grown up in a non-natural or partly non-natural environment, and spent their early weeks in pots in a greenhouse, as can—to take an obvious case—the flowers in one's garden. In any case, Carlson's natural environment model seems skewed to the appreciation of inanimate objects, or living natural objects that lack the power of locomotion. Creatures capable of movement have no natural position in their environment of creation and need not, and often do not, remain in it—as with birds, who emerge from their eggs and leave their nests (in one sense their environments of creation) and move around in the atmosphere and on the surface of the earth.

The second problem of scope concerns not the scope of the model, but the scope of the knowledge relevant to the aesthetic appreciation of nature. Carlson's thesis is that common-sense/natural-scientific knowledge of nature is essential to the aesthetic appreciation of nature. But how much knowledge about a natural item is relevant? If not all, what makes a piece of knowledge relevant or de rigueur for the item's aesthetic appreciation? For instance, what knowledge of the sun and its relation to the earth (the sun's exact or approximate distance from the earth, say) is relevant to the appreciation of a sunset, and in virtue of what is this knowledge relevant? On the one hand, it is clear that not everything that is true of a natural item needs to be understood in order to appreciate it aesthetically as the natural item it is. A flower is the sexual organ of a plant. But to judge a flower to be a beautiful flower it is not necessary to know its function as the sexual organ of a plant, let alone to appreciate it with respect to how well it performs that natural function.[16] On the other hand, it is clear that scientific knowledge *can* enhance the aesthetic appreciation of nature.[17] The effectiveness of Carlson's claim that knowledge of what is standard for natural things of a certain kind will affect the aesthetic properties an item of that kind appears to possess can be conceded:

---

[16] Does it matter, from the aesthetic point of view, what the natural function of the stripes of a zebra is—something there is, I believe, no scientific consensus about?

[17] See Essay 1, §7.

the aesthetic qualities which natural objects and landscapes appear to have depend upon how they are perceived. The rorqual whale is a graceful and majestic mammal. However, if it were perceived as a fish, it would appear more lumbering, somewhat oafish, perhaps even a bit clumsy (maybe somewhat like the basking shark). Similarly the graceful and even elegant moose would seem an awkward deer; the charming, cute woodchuck, a massive and awe-inspiring brown rat; the delicate sunflower, a stiff and stodgy daisy. (Carlson 1984: 26–7)

But this does not go far enough: all it shows is the aesthetic relevance of a certain sort of category of nature that an item is perceived as instantiating and it does not engage with the issue of what the distinction is between aesthetically relevant and irrelevant or essential and inessential knowledge of nature. Carlson appears not to recognize this lacuna in his account.[18]

As an illustration of this deficiency in Carlson's account, Robert Stecker (1997) has responded in the following way to Carlson's use of Hepburn's example of a tidal basin, the wide expanse of sand and mud which appears to have different aesthetic qualities depending on whether it is perceived as just a beach or as also a tidal basin. The shore of a tidal basin can be appreciated in three ways, none of which is ill-founded: as beach, as seabed, and as sometimes beach/ sometimes seabed. And, although the last is more 'complete' than the first two since it comprehends each of these, there is no compelling reason to prefer the more complete conception, which might, but well might not, enhance one's appreciation. Furthermore:

The more complete conception can still be supplemented indefinitely with knowledge of the physics of tides, the ecosystems of the basin, and additional facts from biology, chemistry and geology ... Nature does not guide us in selecting among this possible information, since encompassing all these facts, it is indifferent about which we mine in pursuit of aesthetic enjoyment. (398)

For Carlson the aesthetic qualities that an item actually possesses are those that it appears to possess (to the right perceiver, under the right conditions) when it is perceived in its correct category; the correct category in which to perceive the expanse of sand and mud is the category of tidal basin; accordingly, the quality of the expanse

---

[18] It is a common weakness of advocates of the view that scientific knowledge is essential to the proper aesthetic appreciation of the natural world not to provide any criteria for determining, for particular natural objects or phenomena, which knowledge enhances aesthetic appreciation.

of sand and mud is not just that of wild, glad emptiness, but of wild, glad emptiness tempered by a disturbing weirdness (Carlson 1984). Note that although the expanse of sand and mud appears to have different qualities when perceived in the categories *beach* and *tidal basin*, the categories are not incompatible, each of them is *a* correct category—the category *only a beach, never a seabed* would be an incorrect category—and the qualities are related in this way: the second is the first with an additional feature, a qualifying characteristic (if this is how the idea of 'being tempered by' is intended to be understood). Accordingly, in itself the example is relatively unproblematic for Carlson: what would be deeply problematic would be a case in which the qualities the item appears to possess when perceived in two correct categories are incompatible. Nevertheless, Carlson shows no awareness of the fact that both beach and tidal basin are correct categories and appears to select as the correct category the more encompassing one, simply because it is more encompassing.

Stecker draws the conclusion that 'it is not clear that knowledge of nature can perform the same function as that of art', namely that of delimiting aesthetically relevant knowledge. But the notion of delimiting aesthetically relevant knowledge of nature is ambiguous and there are two questions that must be distinguished (focusing for simplicity on natural objects). On the one hand, there is an issue about what *can* properly figure in the aesthetic appreciation of a particular natural object: Are there facts about a natural object that are irrelevant to its aesthetic appreciation as natural, i.e. that could not constitute part of its aesthetic appeal or inform its aesthetic appreciation? On the other, there is an issue about what *must* figure in that appreciation if the appreciation is not to be defective, imperfect, shallow, or in some other way inadequate: Is there a set of facts about a natural object, each of which is essential to its full aesthetic appreciation, no fact outside the set being relevant? Stecker's conclusion gives a negative answer to the second question. But this does not imply a negative answer to the first, which should in fact receive a positive answer, although it is not easy to explain why various kinds of fact are disqualified from figuring in the aesthetic appreciation of a natural item (Hepburn 1996).[19]

---

[19] See Essay 1, §7.

(iv) Noël Carroll (1993) has advanced an *arousal model*, not as a replacement for the natural-environment model, but as one coexisting with it, each of the models applying to some but not all of those responses to the natural world that constitute aesthetic appreciation of it, the two models sometimes overlapping. The model is simply that of being emotionally moved by nature, of emotions being appropriately aroused by nature, not all such emotions being rooted in a cognitive component containing a scientific category as part of its content. For example:

we may find ourselves standing under a thundering waterfall and be excited by its grandeur; or standing barefooted amidst a silent arbor, softly carpeted with layers of decaying leaves, a sense of repose and homeyness may be aroused in us. (245)

When we are overwhelmed and excited by the grandeur of the towering cascade of water we focus on certain aspects of the natural expanse—'the palpable force of the cascade, its height, the volume of water, the way it alters the surrounding atmosphere, etc'—a focusing that does not require any special scientific, or even common-sense, ecological knowledge. And being exhilarated by grandeur is an appropriate response to what is grand. Hence, there is a form of aesthetic appreciation of nature that does not conform to the natural environment model.[20] Moreover, so Carroll argues, this mode of aesthetic appreciation of nature is such that (a) it can yield the conclusion that aesthetic judgements about nature can be objectively correct—a conclusion that Carlson appears to believe can be yielded only by the natural-environment model—because aesthetic judgements based on or expressive of emotional responses to appropriate natural objects possess objectivity, and (b) there is no good reason to accept that it must be a less deep appreciation of nature than one informed by natural history, if depth of response is a matter of intensity and 'thoroughgoingness' of involvement.

Carroll neglects to specify that for an emotion appropriately aroused by nature to constitute aesthetic appreciation of nature the emotional response must be an aesthetic response, not every emotional response to nature being an aesthetic response, let alone

[20] Carroll understands Carlson's natural-environment model to require systematic knowledge of natural processes, so that the common-sense knowledge that is involved in the aesthetic appreciation of the waterfall—that what is falling down is water, for example—is not common-sense knowledge of nature of the kind the natural-environment model demands.

an aesthetic response to nature as nature; and not only does he not provide an account of what makes a response an aesthetic response, some of his examples of emotional responses to nature are definitely not aesthetic responses. But these defects are easily rectified.[21]

Carlson (1995) does not press this point and adopts a different tack: prescinding from the question of what constitutes an aesthetic response to an item, he focuses on the notion of *appreciation*.[22] Since the appreciation of an item requires some information about it, correct appreciation of an item requires knowledge of that item. It follows that if a certain piece, or number of pieces, of knowledge is required for proper appreciation of nature, then an emotional response not based on the required knowledge is not a truly appreciative response. It is clear that the arousal model does not exclude whatever knowledge is required for appropriate appreciation of nature from being the basis of an emotional reaction to nature that constitutes aesthetic appreciation of nature. The question, therefore, is whether it incorrectly deems cases of emotional response to nature that are not based on the required knowledge to be instances of appropriate appreciation of nature.

This depends on what knowledge is required for aesthetic appreciation of nature. The natural-environment model maintains that the required knowledge is 'that which is provided by the natural sciences and their common-sense predecessors and analogues', whereas the arousal model rejects such knowledge as being required for appropriate appreciation of nature. Carlson here makes two moves. The first exploits a feature of one of Carroll's examples in an attempt to show that the arousal model collapses into the natural-environment model. The example is one of being moved by the grandeur of a blue whale, 'its size, its force, the amount of water it displaces'. But knowledge of the amount of water a blue whale displaces—by which it is clear that Carroll means not the precise amount of water, but only that the amount is large—is 'if not exactly straightforwardly scientific, at least the product of the commonsense predecessors or analogues of science', so that appreciation of the whale, grounded partly in the amount of water it displaces, is based on knowledge of the kind required by the natural-environment

---

[21] See Essay 1, §5.

[22] Carlson's (1995) account of appreciation is contested by Godlovitch (1997), but that critique is effectively countered by Carlson (1997).

model, 'even though that knowledge comes from the commonsense end of the spectrum ranging from science to its commonsense analogues'. Similarly, Carlson is inclined to regard the knowledge that what, in Carroll's waterfall example, is cascading down is water as the product of the common-sense predecessors and analogues of natural science. And although he is prepared to concede that perhaps this is not 'systematic knowledge of nature's working', this is, for him, a negligible concession. For Carlson concludes that instances of appreciation of nature in accordance with the arousal model that are based on knowledge only of this kind are at best minimal, so that, as far as the knowledge element of appropriate appreciation of nature is concerned, there is no significant difference between the arousal and natural-environment models, the first focusing on the most minimal, the second on the fuller and richer levels of such appreciation.

It will be clear that Carlson's response runs up against the problematic issue of the extent of aesthetically relevant knowledge of nature. And, since not every kind of appreciation is aesthetic appreciation, a response based on a deeper, as opposed to a shallower, appreciation (in the sense of understanding) of the nature of a natural item is not automatically indicative of a deeper, as opposed to a shallower, aesthetic response to that item, one that is the manifestation of a fuller and richer appreciation of that item from the aesthetic point of view. Without an account of what it is for appreciation to be specifically aesthetic and a principled distinction between knowledge that is relevant and knowledge that is not relevant to the aesthetic appreciation of a natural thing, Carlson cannot press home his critique of the arousal model.

Carlson does make some claims about what is involved in specifically aesthetic appreciation in (Carlson 2000). He requires serious appropriate aesthetic appreciation to be founded on knowledge of what kind of thing the object of appreciation is and what its properties are, this knowledge informing the perception of the object and directing behaviour towards it. Furthermore, the knowledge required for appropriate aesthetic appreciation includes, for all objects, knowledge of the object's 'history of production', that is, the explanation of how the object of appreciation came to be as it is, and, for those objects that have been designed to perform a function or fulfil a purpose, knowledge of that function or purpose; that is, why it came to be as it is.

Any conception of aesthetic appreciation that acknowledges that it can be appropriate or inappropriate needs an account of what determines whether a fact about a particular item is relevant or irrelevant to the appropriate aesthetic appreciation of that item. Leaving aside what a natural object presents to the senses (and what exactly this includes), something that is deemed relevant by all conceptions of aesthetic appreciation, Carlson regards as aesthetically relevant the object's kind or category (and those of the natural items it contains, if, as is true of a landscape, it does so), its 'history of production', and its function or purpose, if it has one. By their being aesthetically relevant he means that information about these facts (and perhaps no other) is necessary for appropriate aesthetic appreciation of the object; and his position is that appreciation informed by scientific categorization and awareness of 'history of production' and function is thereby enhanced and deepened.

But this suggestion about the scope of aesthetically relevant facts lacks a really solid basis, is not fully worked out, and, as it stands, appears open to counter examples. First, in order for the suggestion to be convincing, an account is needed of what is common (and perhaps peculiar) to these sorts of fact in virtue of which they are (supposedly) aesthetically relevant, such an account ideally being derived from a characterization of the nature of the aesthetic, something Carlson does not attempt to provide. And whereas the aesthetic relevance of an object's type is definitively established by showing that it is a determinant of the aesthetic qualities the object can truly be said to possess as an instance of that type, the aesthetic relevance of a natural object's 'history of production' is not supported by a similar or equally powerful consideration. (Significant differences between nature and art preclude the aesthetic relevance of a work of art's 'history of production' from being a sufficient reason.) Second, the suggestion is shrouded in a penumbra of vagueness. For, just as not every aspect of a work of art's history of production is relevant to its aesthetic appreciation, not all information about how a natural phenomenon came to be what it is is relevant to its aesthetic appreciation. Accordingly, the suggestion will become definite only if those aspects that are so relevant are identified; and an explanation is needed of why they (and no others) are relevant. Third, there appear to be many instances of the aesthetic appreciation of nature where it is unnecessary to have any substantial knowledge, perhaps any knowledge at all, of the 'history of production' of an object of appreciation. Consider, for example, one of Carlson's fundamental paradigms of aesthetic appreciation, the appreciation of the grace of a bird in flight. It is clear that one does not need to know the explanation of the bird's growth inside the shell from which it emerged and of how the bird's skeleton and feathers developed from their fledgling state in order to appreciate the bird's graceful flight. Nor is it obvious that an understanding of the bird's origin, formation, and development is required for any other aspect of the appropriate aesthetic appreciation of the adult bird.

(v) In his advocacy of an acentric natural aesthetic Stan Godlovitch has proposed an *aloofness model* (Godlovitch 1994). An acentric natural aesthetic is the aesthetic correlative and essential ground of acentric environmentalism. Environmentalism is the view that nature needs protecting. Unlike centric forms of environmentalism, which attempt to justify the protection of the natural environment on instrumental, consequentialist, or purely utilitarian grounds, preserving terrestrial nature for the earth's inhabitants, acentric environmentalism, which 'is rooted in the belief that we are prima facie bound not to interfere in any of the world undefined by culture whether or not it supports life', ascribes a non-instrumental value, an intrinsic non-moral worth, to all of nature indiscriminately, privileging nothing (the animate over the inanimate, for example). Accordingly, acentric environmentalism is concerned to protect nature 'as it is and not merely as it is for us' or for any other sentient creatures. Hence, it does not locate this value in beings that have a point of view: it does not privilege any special interests or centres of concern. An acentric environmentalism is therefore dependent on an acentric natural aesthetic.

An acentric natural aesthetic prescribes the appreciation of nature through an acentric aesthetic: the aesthetic appreciation of nature 'as a whole', 'on its own terms', 'as itself', 'as it is', must be acentric, which requires a particular (acentric) attitude to nature, one that is indifferent to human scale and perspective. The adoption of an acentric aesthetic for the aesthetic appreciation of nature implies that a centric (e.g. anthropocentric) natural aesthetic has an 'unavoidably arbitrary' character. For what we find aesthetically offensive about the violation of nature (wanton environmental destruction) and the degree to which we do so—more generally, our aesthetic concerns about or preferences for nature—is limited by our spatial and temporal scale, which, like our perceptual capacities and their limits, are irrelevant from 'the view from nowhere'. For an acentric aesthetic, on the other hand, there is something aesthetically offensive about any wanton environmental destruction, no matter how this relates to our biological limits. Transcending the temporal and spatial limits of human life, attributing an intrinsic non-moral value to all of nature, however small, large, brief, or long, implies rejecting 'the sensuous surface of our common perceptual world' as the basis of aesthetic judgement of nature. This transcendence involves the recognition 'that Nature is, for us, fundamentally inaccessible and ultimately alien', '[the] aloof, [the] distant, [the] unknowable, [the] Other', 'for which we have, in principle, no significance', a 'mystery of aloofness'. Since nothing in nature 'as a whole' has any special significance, to adopt an acentric natural aesthetic we must not regard nature anthropocentrically (or biocentrically) but have 'a sense of being outside, of not belonging' and of insignificance, so that we can recognize 'proper impersonality, true indifference and autonomy which are Nature's principal marks'. In other words, the fitting attitude towards nature 'as a whole' is (not respect or reverence or love or awe or wonder, but) aloofness: 'Nature is aloof, and it is this aloofness we [must] come, not so much to understand or revere, as to attempt to mirror or match'—matching the 'mystery of aloofness', a mystery that cannot have a solution, 'in a state of appreciative incomprehension'.

One essential element of Godlovitch's position is the alleged necessity of nature's unknowability ('the necessity of the unknowable'), the idea that nature 'as a whole', nature *qua* nature, must elude our science, that no matter what science explains about nature there will always be further unexplained issues, that science's goal of demystifying the world cannot be achieved, so that we are faced by nature with a mystery to which there is no (ultimate) solution. This is not the long-familiar thought that science is unable to explain why there is anything at all and why the laws of nature are as they are. Rather, Godlovitch contrasts science's pursuit of nature's foundation, of what the world is ultimately made of and the laws that govern it, with 'the image of worlds within worlds without end captured in Fractal Ontology where each level reveals as much detail and complexity as the level above; where there are no ultimate simples, no basic constituents, no ontic base-ment'. But the possibility of fractal ontology does not imply its actuality, and it is only if nature is actually endlessly 'deep' that it will be impossible for science fully to demystify the world (in the sense at issue).

However, even if nature is at bottom unfathomable, even if it is impossible to plumb its infinite depths, it does not follow that our aesthetic attitude towards natural things should always be the same, and, in particular, that it should be an attitude of aloofness, mirroring the ultimate mysteriousness of everything in nature. Godlovitch slips easily between the idea that nature is at bottom unfathomable, ultimately mysterious, and the idea that nature is 'categorically other than us', something 'of which we were never a part'. And this second idea yields the conception of nature as being alien and aloof, nature's aloofness requiring a matching aloofness in our attitude to it—'a sense of being outside, of not belonging'—if our attitude towards it is to be one that expresses nature's intrinsic, non-consequential value. But, first, it would not follow from nature's ultimate unfathomability that we are not part of nature, that we are outside it, that we do not belong to it. Rather, we would ourselves, if part of nature, be at bottom unfathomable. And of course we *are* natural objects, composed of matter like other natural objects, being no more distant from nature than any other animate or inanimate things (Hepburn 1996: 252). Godlovitch suspects that we are more distant than other species from nature because he cannot imagine being more distant than we are. This thought follows hard upon his claim that although we can to a certain extent understand 'the experiential world' of other species, for example their hunger, pain, and fear, we are 'peculiarly ill-equipped to comprehend' 'the silent void of waves and rocks and fire'. But, of course, we are not 'peculiarly ill-equipped', for there is nothing to comprehend, other than the physical nature of waves, rocks, and trees, the way they are formed and develop, the physical forces they are vulnerable to, and so on. It seems as if Godlovitch derives our supposed distance from nature from the fact of our experiencing the world—something absent in most of nature—and our ability to reflect on the phenom-enology of experiential states and to think about the world—an ability lacking in any other terrestrial sentient species. But difference is not the same as, and does not imply, distance. So the idea that the proper aesthetic attitude towards nature is one of aloofness receives no support from the idea that such an attitude matches or mirrors nature's aloofness, that is distance, from us. And the putative ultimate mysteriousness of nature is not in itself sufficient to warrant the claim that the proper aesthetic attitude towards nature is one of aloofness: not only are there more fitting attitudes towards ineradicable mysteriousness, in fact there is a curious mismatch between aloofness and mysteriousness, since the attitude in no way constitutes a suitable response to its object.[23]

This leaves two matters unattended to: the intrinsic non-moral worth attributed by acentric environmentalism to all of nature indiscriminately, and the alleged arbitrariness of an anthropocentric natural aesthetic. They can be dealt with very briefly. First, what is wrong with wanton environmental destruction as such, which means even when no habitat is jeopardized, is just that it is wanton, expressing nothing better than delight in destruction. So wanton environmental destruction does not need to be thought of as being aesthetically offensive and acentric environmentalism does not need to locate an intrinsic non-moral worth in nature. And, second, since Godlovitch's argument concerning the alleged arbitrariness of a centric natural aesthetic hinges on just this mistaken claim—'If we were giants, crushing a rock monument, even a stony moon, would be no more aesthetically offensive than flattening the odd sand castle is to us now'—it falls with it.

4.10.   A CHIMERICAL QUEST

If none of the proposed models of the appropriate aesthetic appreciation of nature is adequate, what should take their place? Given the role that such a model is intended to perform, the correct answer

[23] Carlson, who regards Godlovitch's position as more a religion of nature worship than a model of [at least a dimension of] the appropriate aesthetic appreciation of nature (Carlson 1995), himself embraces the conclusion that, because nature is 'distinct from and beyond humankind, something essentially alien', 'Our appreciative response is to a mystery we will seemingly never fully comprehend . . . in appreciating nature we are aware that the object is alien, a mystery, and therefore ultimately beyond our appreciation and beyond our understanding, our judgment, our mastery' (Carlson 1993).

is, I believe, 'Nothing': the fact that the aesthetic appreciation of nature is endowed with a freedom denied to the appreciation of art renders the search for a model of the aesthetic appreciation of nature (in particular, the natural environment) that will indicate what is to be appreciated and how it is to be appreciated—something we have a good grasp of in the case of works of art—a chimerical quest. In the case of art, Carlson writes: 'We know what to appreciate in that we can distinguish a work and its parts from that which is not it nor a part of it...And...we can distinguish its aesthetically relevant aspects from its aspects without such relevance'. And we know how to appreciate a work of art in that we know whether to look or listen, from what distance, whether to remain in one spot or to move around, and so on. The assumption underlying the search for a model of the aesthetic appreciation of nature is that some counterpart of our knowledge of art is needed that in the case of nature (or the natural environment) will answer the what and how questions about nature that we know so well how to answer in the case of a work of art. But, first, there is no counterpart problem about what to appreciate in nature: in general we need no special knowledge to be able to distinguish a natural item and its parts from any other natural thing and no aspect of a natural item that is capable of being appreciated aesthetically is properly deemed an aesthetically irrelevant aspect of the item; and we are free to consider any natural item either in itself or in the context of a larger ensemble (the ecosystem to which it belongs, for example), or to focus not on an individual natural item but on an array or a group of natural items (a sky-scape, or a flock, for instance). And, second, there are no constraints imposed on manner of appreciation—what actions to perform and mode of perception to engage in—in virtue of the natural category an item belongs to that parallel the constraints imposed by categories of art. Accordingly, there is no such thing as the appropriate foci of aesthetic significance in the natural environment or the appropriate boundaries of the setting. The answer to the question, 'In the case of nature (i) what is to be aesthetically appreciated and (ii) how is it to be aesthetically appreciated?' is just this: (i) Whatever is available in nature for aesthetic appreciation (as nature), (ii) in whatever manner or manners it is possible to appreciate it aesthetically (as nature). The mistaken search for a model of the correct or appropriate aesthetic appreciation of nature reflects a lack of recognition of

REFERENCES

ALLISON, HENRY (2001). *Kant's Theory of Taste*. Cambridge: Cambridge University Press.

ARISTOTLE (2001). *On the Parts of Animals*, trans. James G. Lennox. Oxford: Clarendon Press.

BEARDSLEY, MONROE C. (1970). 'The Aesthetic Point of View', in Howard Kiefer and Milton Munitz (eds.), *Perspectives in Education, Religion, and the Arts*. Albany: SUNY Press, 219–37. Repr. in Beardsley's *The Aesthetic Point of View*. Ithaca and London: Cornell University Press, 1982, 15–34.

BEISER, FREDERICK (1998). 'Schiller, Johann Christoph Friedrich von', in Michael Kelly (ed.), *Encyclopedia of Aesthetics*. New York: Oxford University Press, iv. 224–9.

BERLEANT, ARNOLD (1993). 'The Aesthetics of Art and Nature', in Salim Kemal and Ivan Gaskell (eds.), *Landscape, Natural Beauty and the Arts*. Cambridge: Cambridge University Press, 228–43.

BRADLEY, A. C. (1909). 'The Sublime', in his *Oxford Lectures on Poetry*. London: Macmillan, 37–65.

BUDD, MALCOLM (2001a). 'Wollheim on Correspondence, Projective Properties and Expressive Perception', in Rob van Gerwen (ed.), *Richard Wollheim on the Art of Painting: Art as Representation and Expression*. Cambridge: Cambridge University Press, 101–11.

—— (2001b). 'The Pure Judgement of Taste as an Aesthetic Reflective Judgement'. *British Journal of Aesthetics*, 41/3 (July 2001), 247–60.

BURKE, EDMUND (1958). *A Philosophical Enquiry into the Origin of our Ideas of the Sublime and Beautiful*, ed. J. T. Boulton. London: Routledge and Kegan Paul.

CARLSON, ALLEN (1976). 'Environmental Aesthetics and the Dilemma of Aesthetic Education'. *Journal of Aesthetic Education*, 10/2, 69–82.

—— (1977). 'On the Possibility of Quantifying Scenic Beauty'. *Landscape Planning*, 4/2 131–72.

—— (1979a). 'Appreciation and the Natural Environment'. *Journal of Aesthetics and Art Criticism*, 37/3, 267–75.

—— (1979b). 'Formal Qualities in the Natural Environment'. *Journal of Aesthetic Education*, 13/3, 99–114.

—— (1981). 'Nature, Aesthetic Judgment, and Objectivity'. *Journal of Aesthetics and Art Criticism*, 40/1, 15–27.

—— (1984). 'Nature and Positive Aesthetics'. *Environmental Ethics*, 6: 5–34.

CARLSON, ALLEN (1986). 'Saito on the Correct Aesthetic Appreciation of Nature'. *Journal of Aesthetic Education*, 20/2, 85–93.

—— (1992). 'Environmental Aesthetics', in David Cooper (ed.), *A Companion to Aesthetics*. Oxford: Basil Blackwell, 142–4.

—— (1993). 'Appreciating Art and Appreciating Nature', in Salim Kemal and Ivan Gaskell (eds.), *Landscape, Natural Beauty and the Arts*. Cambridge: Cambridge University Press, 199–227.

—— (1995). 'Nature, Aesthetic Appreciation, and Knowledge'. *Journal of Aesthetics and Art Criticism*, 53/4, 393–400.

—— (1997). 'Appreciating Godlovitch'. *Journal of Aesthetics and Art Criticism*, 55/1, 55–7.

—— (1998). 'Nature: Contemporary Thought', in Michael Kelly (ed.), *Encyclopedia of Aesthetics*. New York: Oxford University Press, ii. 346–9.

—— (2000). *Aesthetics and the Environment*. London and New York: Routledge.

CARROLL, NOËL (1993). 'On Being Moved by Nature: Between Religion and Natural History', in Salim Kemal and Ivan Gaskell (eds.), *Landscape, Natural Beauty and the Arts*. Cambridge: Cambridge University Press, 244–66.

CRANE, TIM (1992). 'The Nonconceptual Content of Experience', in Tim Crane (ed.), *The Contents of Experience*. Cambridge: Cambridge University Press, 136–57.

DANTO, ARTHUR (1983). *The Transfiguration of the Commonplace*. London: Harvard University Press.

DARWIN, CHARLES (1929). *The Origin of Species* (last (6th) edn.). London: Watts.

DAVIES, STEPHEN (1991). *Definitions of Art*. Ithaca and London: Cornell University Press.

—— (1994). *Musical Meaning and Expression*. Ithaca and London: Cornell University Press.

EVANS, GARETH (1982). *The Varieties of Reference*. Oxford: Clarendon Press.

GODLOVITCH, STAN (1994). 'Icebreakers: Environmentalism and Natural Aesthetics'. *Journal of Applied Philosophy*, 11/1, 15–30.

—— (1997). 'Carlson on Appreciation'. *Journal of Aesthetics and Art Criticism*, 55/1, 53–5.

—— (1998a). 'Valuing Nature and the Autonomy of Natural Aesthetics'. *British Journal of Aesthetics*, 38/2, 180–97.

—— (1998b). 'Evaluating Nature Aesthetically'. *Journal of Aesthetics and Art Criticism*, 56/2, 113–25.

GUYER, PAUL (1996). *Kant and the Experience of Freedom*. Cambridge: Cambridge University Press.

HARGROVE, EUGENE (1989). *Foundations of Environmental Ethics*. Englewood Cliffs, NJ: Prentice Hall.

HEGEL, G. W. F. (1975). *Aesthetics: Lectures on Fine Art*, trans. T. M. Knox. Oxford: Clarendon Press.

HEPBURN, RONALD (1966). 'Contemporary Aesthetics and the Neglect of Natural Beauty', in B. Williams and A. Montefiori (eds.), *British Analytical Philosophy*. London: Routledge and Kegan Paul, 285–310.

—— (1996). 'Data and Theory in Aesthetics: Philosophical Understanding and Misunderstanding', in Anthony O'Hear (ed.), *Verstehen and Humane Understanding*. Cambridge: Cambridge University Press, 235–52.

—— (1998). 'Nature Humanised: Nature Respected'. *Environmental Values*, 7: 267–79.

HUME, DAVID (1960). *A Treatise of Human Nature*, ed. L. A. Selby-Bigge. Oxford: Clarendon Press.

—— (1961). *An Enquiry Concerning the Principles of Morals*, ed. L. A. Selby-Bigge. Oxford: Clarendon Press.

KANT, IMMANUEL (1974). *Anthropology From a Pragmatic Point of View*, trans. Mary J. Gregor. The Hague: Martinus Nijhoff.

—— (1991). *The Metaphysics of Morals*, trans. Mary Gregor. Cambridge: Cambridge University Press.

—— (1992). *Lectures on Logic*, trans. and ed. J. Michael Young. Cambridge: Cambridge University Press.

—— (1993). *Critique of Practical Reason*, trans. Lewis White Beck. New York: Macmillan.

LEOPOLD, ALDO (1989). *A Sand County Almanac*. Oxford: Oxford University Press.

MCDOWELL, JOHN (1994). *Mind and World*. Cambridge, Mass.: Harvard University Press.

MILLER, MARA (1993). *The Garden as an Art*. Albany, NY: State University of New York Press.

NICOLSON, MARJORIE HOPE (1959). *Mountain Gloom and Mountain Glory: The Development of the Aesthetics of the Infinite*. Ithaca, NY: Cornell University Press.

PASSMORE, JOHN (1980). *Man's Responsibility for Nature* (2nd edn.). London: Duckworth.

PEACOCKE, CHRISTOPHER (1993). *A Study of Concepts*. Cambridge, Mass.: MIT Press.

ROLSTON III, HOLMES (1988). *Environmental Ethics*. Philadelphia, Pa.: Temple University Press.

—— (1998). 'Aesthetic Experience in Forests'. *Journal of Aesthetics and Art Criticism*, 56/2, 157–66.

ROSS, STEPHANIE (1998). *What Gardens Mean*. London and Chicago, Ill.: University of Chicago Press.

SAITO, YURIKO (1984). 'Is there a Correct Aesthetic Appreciation of Nature?'. *Journal of Aesthetic Education*, 18/4, 35–46.

152 References

SAITO, YURIKO (1998), 'The Aesthetics of Unscenic Nature'. *Journal of Aesthetics and Art Criticism*, 56/2, 101–11.

SAVILE, ANTHONY (1982). *The Test of Time*. Oxford: Clarendon Press.

SCHILLER, FRIEDRICH (1951). *Über Naive und Sentimentalische Dichtung*, ed. William F. Mainland. Oxford: Basil Blackwell.

——(1982). *On the Aesthetic Education of Man: In a Series of Letters*. Oxford: Clarendon Press.

SCHOPENHAUER, ARTHUR (1969). *The World as Will and Representation*, trans. E. F. J. Payne. New York: Dover.

——(1974). *Parerga and Paralipomena*, trans. E. F. J. Payne. Clarendon Press: Oxford.

SIBLEY, FRANK (2001*a*). 'Aesthetic Judgements: Pebbles, Faces, and Fields of Litter', in his *Approach to Aesthetics*. Oxford: Clarendon Press, 176–89.

——(2001*b*), 'Arts or the Aesthetic—Which Comes First?', in his *Approach to Aesthetics*. Oxford: Clarendon Press, 135–41.

SONTAG, SUSAN (1964). 'Notes on Camp'. *Partisan Review*, 31: 515–30. Repr. in her *Against Interpretation*. London: Andre Deutsch, 1987, 275–92.

STECKER, ROBERT (1997). 'The Correct and the Appropriate in the Appreciation of Nature'. *British Journal of Aesthetics*, 37/4, 393–402.

TUAN, YI-FU (1990). *Topophilia*. New York: Columbia University Press.

WALTON, KENDALL (1970). 'Categories of Art'. *Philosophical Review*, 79/3, 334–67.

WOLLHEIM, RICHARD (1980). *Art and Its Objects* (2nd edn.). Cambridge: Cambridge University Press.

——(1991). 'Correspondence, Projective Properties, and Expression in the Arts', in Ivan Gaskell and Salim Kemal (eds.), *The Language of Art History*. Cambridge: Cambridge University Press, 51–66. Repr. in his *The Mind and Its Depths*. Cambridge, Mass. and London: Harvard University Press, 1993, 144–58.

INDEX

Index

DATE DUE
